MAMALITA

An Adoption Memoir

Jessica O'Dwyer

SEAL PRESS

MAMALITA
An Adoption Memoir

Published by
Seal Press
A Member of the Perseus Books Group
1700 Fourth Street
Berkeley, California

Library of Congress Cataloging-in-Publication Data

O'Dwyer, Jessica, 1958-
  Mamalita : an adoption memoir / by Jessica O'Dwyer.
    p. cm.
  ISBN 978-1-58005-334-1
1. Intercountry adoption—Guatemala—Case studies. 2. Intercountry adoption—United States—Case studies. 3. Adoptive parents—United States. I. Title.
  HV875.58.G9O39 2010
  362.734092—dc22
  [B]
                                          2010001781

9 8 7 6 5 4 3 2 1

Cover and interior design by Domini Dragoone
Printed in the United States of America by Edwards Brothers
Distributed by Publishers Group West

A portion of this book was published in the *West Marin Review*, a publication of the Tomales Bay Library Association.

In order to respect the privacy of individuals mentioned in the book, the author has changed some names and altered some details of the story.

For my children and their
other mothers, with love.

CONTENTS

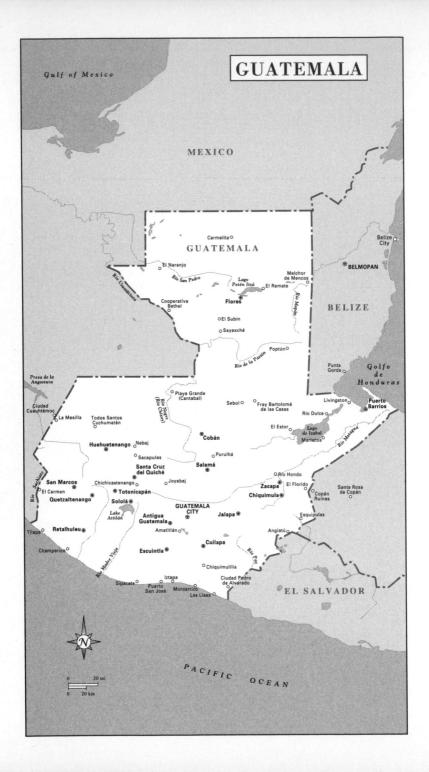

PART ONE

Chapter 1

THE HOTEL LOBBY

I've never given birth, but I know the exact moment when I became a mother: 10:00 AM, September 6, 2002. My husband and I sat huddled on a sofa in the lobby of the Guatemala City Camino Real hotel. On sofas in every direction, other light-skinned American couples cooed over their brown-skinned infants.

Our in-country facilitator, Theodore, strode toward us across the lobby's polished marble floor, his stainless steel Rolex loose around his left wrist. He wasn't Guatemalan but Greek. We had met for the first time that morning.

Behind him was a foster mother. She was dressed in tight designer blue jeans and black leather boots, a pile of pink blankets pressed against her chest. As soon as she reached us, she sat next to me and shifted the bundle to my arms without saying a word.

My heart pounding, I peeked inside.

It wasn't our baby.

I turned the blankets toward my husband, Tim. "Does this look like Stefany Mishell to you?"

This baby had thin tufts of brown hair. Stefany had black hair as thick as yarn. This baby was tiny and frail. Stefany had weighed a robust six pounds ten ounces at birth and was now four months old. And where were her elegantly shaped ears?

The foster mother glanced at Theodore before answering. She seemed to be seeking permission to speak. "*Es* Tiffany Dolores."

"Tiffany Dolores?" I said. "Our baby is Stefany Mishell."

Theodore, perched on the edge of a pinstriped wing chair across from the sofa, jumped up. "This is not your baby," he said.

I passed her back to the foster mother, who began to sing in a soft voice. I didn't want to see this baby, or touch her, or develop any feelings for her unless she was going to be ours. With the edges of my mouth quivering, I put my hand over my heart.

"She's lovely," I said. "But she's not Stefany."

I had fallen in love with Stefany from the single photograph we had of her: skin the color of nutmeg, hair as black as a crow. Brown eyes wide open, scowling at the camera. Her head was turned slightly to one side, and barely visible through her hair was that small, elegant ear.

I scanned the sofas dotted throughout the lobby, trying to see if one of the other couples had been given Stefany. The other Americans were grinning and rubbing noses with their babies.

"I call Yolanda," Theodore said. "We find your baby."

Yolanda was our agency director in Los Angeles who was supposed to relay information about us to Theodore. Before we had left San Francisco, I emailed her every detail: our flight number, our arrival time, our departure date. The one detail I didn't confirm was the name of our baby. Because Yolanda was responsible for completing the paperwork for the U.S. and Guatemalan governments, I assumed she knew that.

Tim and I watched as Theodore hustled the foster mother across the lobby toward the front door. On the sidewalk outside, Theodore snapped open his cell phone and started pushing buttons with one hand. A black-and-white taxi pulled up to the curb and Theodore held onto the cell phone with his chin while he opened the back door. The foster mother climbed inside.

Tim reached over and squeezed my knee. "Think of this as false labor," he said.

I forced a smile. We would have to wait a little longer.

Theodore returned, rubbing his hands together as if trying to get back his circulation. He flopped into the pinstriped wing chair with the ease of someone at home in his living room, which in a sense, he was. According to his business card, his office was the hotel lobby.

"We found your baby." He shook his wrist in an *Ay, ay, ay* gesture with which I would become very familiar. "Yolanda has too many babies to keep track of."

Tim nodded sympathetically. "How long have you two worked together?"

"Six years here. We worked in Romania ten years, but the babies, they cry in the cribs and nobody picks them up. Before that, we owned a Greek restaurant in Hermosa Beach."

He added this nonchalantly, as if owning a restaurant was the normal career path to facilitating international adoptions.

"I hear the food business is brutal," Tim said.

"Nothing compared to this." Theodore shook his wrist again. "You brought the supplies?"

Tim pointed behind the sofa to the eight overstuffed shopping bags.

Yolanda had given us a long list of supplies for the foster mother to use for Stefany: a framed picture of ourselves; a cassette recording of our voices; one hundred eighty disposable diapers; six packages each of wet wipes, diaper rash cream, and shampoo; seven sets of pajamas, onesies, and socks. We brought every item and more. When Tim and I had wrestled our four gigantic suitcases off the lone luggage carousel in Aurora International Airport, we looked as if we were staying for a year, not a short visit over a three-day weekend.

Theodore informed us that Stefany's foster mother—the correct one—lived in a suburb one hour north of Guatemala City. Theodore and Tim invited me to join them in the restaurant for coffee, but I couldn't move from the sofa. I stared across the lobby to the hotel entrance, awaiting my daughter's arrival. My arms ached to hold her.

Bellmen in beige uniforms and tan rubber-soled shoes pushed shiny brass carts stacked high with suitcases. Guatemalan businessmen walked in pairs to the hotel restaurant. The staffers checked in guests swiftly and efficiently. The concierge answered questions with a dazzling smile.

The Camino Real was the most luxurious hotel in Guatemala. The crown jewel of the capital city, it was complete with crystal chandeliers, blue porcelain vases sprouting bunches of flowers, and a polished marble floor as shiny as an ice rink, maintained by a team of cleaners who never stopped swabbing it. Neighboring buildings were protected by cement walls topped with razor wire, and policemen armed with sawed-off shotguns patrolled every street. But inside the Camino Real, all appeared to be in order. American couples rose from the sofas with their babies. They were parents with children now. Families.

Tim and Theodore returned with three coffees on a tray. I poured steamed milk into a thin china cup and stirred with a demitasse spoon. Except for us and the front desk staff and concierge, the lobby was now empty, which was a relief. I had dreaded meeting our baby among so many strangers.

The familiar flavor of warm coffee comforted me. I told myself this was the last cup of coffee I'd drink without knowing Stefany.

Theodore clutched the arms of his chair. "Your baby is here!" He sprang from his seat and race-walked across the floor.

A compact Guatemalan woman carrying the telltale bundle of blankets stood at the front door. Theodore steered her toward us. As they approached, I saw a baby's head covered with so much black hair it looked like she was wearing a beret.

"That's her." I set down my coffee cup unsteadily in the saucer. Tim and I stood.

The foster mother, Lupe Garza, placed the bundle in my arms. The baby felt small, the size and weight of a kitten. Her head fit neatly inside the crook of my elbow. I lowered myself to the sofa, not sure I could remain standing.

I pushed back the blankets from around her face. I recognized her as mine, as ours. I breathed in the sweet smell of her chubby baby cheeks, swept my fingertips along the softness of her brown arm. She was perfect and beautiful, with a high forehead and tiny red lips. Fierce, pure love washed over me as I whispered her name.

She was my daughter, and I was her mother.

How could I have ever known that this was only the beginning?

Every American in the Camino Real lobby had a different reason for adopting. Mine was because I had gone through menopause twelve years earlier, at the age of thirty-two.

When the hot flashes started, I thought I was imagining them. During the day, rivulets of sweat dripped down my legs. At night, my sheets got so drenched I slept on towels.

Still, I never expected my gynecologist to call me to say I was in the throes of early menopause. He had drawn vials of my blood for testing, and the results were conclusive. The condition, called premature ovarian failure, affects one to four percent of women over the age of fifteen. No one really understands why. Whatever the cause, it meant that my body had stopped producing eggs. My chance of becoming pregnant was less than five percent.

In the span of one three-minute phone conversation, everything I ever believed about my life changed. How could I go through life without the experience of someone calling me "Mommy"? Why would I want to? I was one of five children. My sisters each had three. Family meant everything to us. At every holiday—Thanksgiving, Christmas, Easter, Mother's Day—I sat at a table full of nieces and nephews and thought *This is what I want. What else matters?* The ability to create children seemed like a birthright, the definition of being female.

To make matters worse, I was recently divorced from a college beau I married in my mid-twenties. Everything had seemed on track for a baby before thirty, until he left me for one of his colleagues. I was thrust back into the dating world feeling like damaged goods.

Precisely how much information about my infertility should I share with a man? And when? If I told a guy everything soon after we met, he accused me of rushing him to make a decision about the relationship. But if I didn't tell him until later, he accused me of withholding facts.

"You mean you're sterile?" one man asked. "How old are you anyway?" asked another. As tough as those questions were, though, they were a snap compared with the one posed by my last boyfriend: "How can I continue this relationship, knowing the possibility of offspring is denied to me forever?"

It was a fair question, and one I may have asked myself.

Women talk about the wisdom of menopause, a change brought on by the shift in hormones that causes them to view their lives in a new way. Maybe that was what happened to me. After six months of crying almost nonstop, one morning I woke up infused with insight. With extreme clarity, I saw my life as finite, understanding that entire systems in my body could, without warning, break down.

I stopped obsessing about what I couldn't have and began to concentrate on alternatives. Egg donation didn't appeal to me. Millions of babies existed who needed love, and I had an enormous need to love a baby. It didn't matter if we shared genetic material as long as we shared that need. I read every book and article I could find on the subject of adoption and educated myself on the options: domestic, foster care, international.

Since graduating from college in 1980, I had focused on building my career, first in New York City and then in Los Angeles. Now I yearned for a simpler lifestyle. I quit my job in the press office at the L.A. County Museum of Art and found a new one at a smaller museum in San Diego. Although I had grown up at the Jersey shore, my parents and siblings had migrated to San Diego over the years, and I needed to be close to them. I wanted to watch my beloved nieces and nephews grow up.

In my new apartment by the ocean I heard waves crashing and tasted salt in the air. On weekday mornings before reporting for work at San Diego's Museum of Contemporary Art, I rode my bicycle along the beachfront promenade, logging two hundred miles a week with a group of retired Navy captains and ex-SEALs. In the evenings, I jogged on the beach while the sun set. My goal was to become as strong as possible for my new life as an adoptive mother.

But first, I wanted a husband.

Chapter 2

TIM

After I'd been living in San Diego for a few years, I signed up for a five-day, four-hundred mile group bicycle ride through the hills and deserts of San Diego County. A hundred cyclists from around California participated. I didn't sign up because I was daring—timid was more like it—but because the ride took place the week between Christmas and New Year's. That week was hard: the avalanche of cards from friends with children, the office parties to brave solo, the ubiquitous mistletoe.

The first morning I stood in the staging area straddling my bike, wondering what I had gotten myself into. Everyone else seemed to know each other, and they all had monster-sized thighs. There was no way I was going to keep up with this group. But then someone blew a starter's whistle and everyone took off, and the next thing I knew, I was tucked in behind somebody's wheel, being pulled along in the draft.

Around mile twenty, as I hauled myself up a hill, struggling to keep up with the pack, I noticed one of the riders on the side of the road changing a flat tire.

"Need help?" I asked.

He glanced up. Great smile. "No, thanks."

Then, around mile twenty-five, I saw the same rider. "You again?"

Another great smile. Also a wave. Beautiful blue eyes. "Bum tire."

He was cute in an impish way, and he seemed patient and thorough. At night when the group ate dinner at long cafeteria tables, I saw how attentively he listened to people when they talked to him and how his eyes twinkled behind his glasses when he laughed.

I nudged the woman sitting beside me. "Who is that guy?"

"Tim from Marin," she said, identifying him as part of the contingent of riders from up north in Marin County. "Why?"

"No reason," I said. "Just curious."

She laughed. "Nice butt, don't you think?"

The evening before the last day of the ride, the organizers presented gag awards to everyone who participated, culminating in one for "Mr. Nice Guy." The award went to Tim. At the lunch stop the next day, I positioned myself next to him as we waited in the sandwich line at a roadside deli and congratulated him on his Mr. Nice Guy crown.

He groaned. "My whole life it's been the bane of my existence."

"There's nothing wrong with being nice," I assured him, checking to see he if he wore a wedding band. He didn't.

We carried our trays to a picnic table outside and sat beside each other. Tim opened a bag of potato chips and set it between us.

"I've been trying to find a good sourdough bread recipe," he said, biting into his sandwich.

"You bake bread?"

He also grew tomatoes and strawberries and made his own jam. He tended a garden in his Marin backyard, over the Golden Gate Bridge from San Francisco, where he worked as a dermatologist at the University of California. His practice included patients suffering from diseases with names like "pemphigus" and "leishmaniasis" and "notalgia paresthetica." He was divorced with no children, and he liked to travel and dance.

When I told him I worked in a contemporary art museum writing press releases, he said modern art was his favorite. Before he worked for the university, Tim had served as an Army doctor for twelve years. He'd spent hours touring the great museums of Europe. "I developed a real appreciation for German Expressionism," he said.

I had never met a man on a bike ride who knew the difference between contemporary and modern art, who grew tomatoes, made his own jam, and baked bread. In truth, I'd never met a man on a bike ride who didn't spend most of his time telling me about other, better bike rides, and future ones he planned to take.

"I ride in a bike club with a bunch of ex-Navy guys," I said. "That's my connection to the military."

He grabbed my bicep and squeezed. "That's why you're so strong."

Every nerve ending on the surface of my skin tingled.

I knew that when the last leg of the ride was over, Tim was going to return to his life in San Francisco, five hundred miles away. But I'd been single long enough to know how rare our chemistry was. There was a naturalness between us, as if we were continuing a conversation we had started a long time ago instead of just beginning one. Sitting beside him, I was giddy and lightheaded. My cheeks felt warm; I couldn't stop blushing. I wanted to know everything about him.

Before we got back on our bikes—and breaking every rule about being mysterious and playing hard-to-get—I blurted out that there was one more thing Tim might want to know about me: I couldn't have children.

"Just as an FYI," I added.

Tim nodded. "That must be hard for you."

I looked straight into his blue eyes, trying to see all the way through to the inner workings of his mind. "I'd like to adopt."

He emptied a cup of ice into his water bottle before answering. "Adoption is a viable option for a lot of people."

"A lot of people, but not you. Right?" I was already picturing myself riding away alone with my head tucked down.

He touched my arm again, pulling me back from wherever I had gone to protect myself. "Don't put words in my mouth. The truth is, I've never been a big believer in the biological imperative to reproduce myself directly."

"Oh, really?" I said. "How interesting."

Perhaps he wasn't a big believer in the biological imperative to reproduce himself. But after the series of heartbreaks I'd been through, how could I be sure? It was easy to say you didn't believe in something as long as it didn't apply to you. Ask any of my previous boyfriends.

"Is that why you never had children?" I pulled my arm back closer to my side.

Tim sealed the top of his water bottle, shaking it lightly to double-check it was closed. "I was married sixteen years," Tim said. "It just never happened." He must have noticed the way my face fell because he added, "That isn't the reason we broke up. But it's why I don't have children."

Every week for the next three months, Tim express-mailed me a package of homemade bread. Grain spiced with cardamom, carrot flecked with raisins, poppy seed on rye. Tucked inside each was a note: The water in the bay glittered when he rode over the bridge; the soil was rich as he turned it over in his garden, preparing for spring planting; a cloud formation at sunset was the same shade of pink as my cheeks.

I opened the packages cautiously, as if they were something I had to stand back from, a connection too hot to touch. Anyone could write a nice letter, I reminded myself even as I read his over and over, relishing his description of my freckles as "forbidden fruit" and cherishing his pet name for me, the "Maximum Fox." He assembled Top Ten lists of why I was special, clipped articles from the newspaper about appealing art exhibitions we should go see, marked up maps with bike routes we could ride together when I came to visit. I responded via email with short, chatty notes about my job and bike rides, terrified of the intimacy of writing by hand. I was afraid that if I put pen to paper, I might reveal my true feelings for him—the way I appreciated his compassion and sensitivity, his curiosity and intellect, his thoughtfulness. Somehow I might have let slip that I was falling in love.

In March, Tim was invited to lecture in San Diego. The date coincided with a reception at my museum, and I invited him to stop by when he finished. He'd never seen me in anything other than biking shorts or sweat pants, and I was afraid he might not recognize me in my black dress and pearls. But he did, and he hugged me hard in the middle of the atrium.

"I can't stop thinking about you," he whispered in my ear. "You're the love of my life."

I started laughing and crying, astonished. We kissed for the first time.

We dated long-distance for a year before I moved to Tim's house in Marin. By then, his love for me convinced him he was also ready to adopt. When I told my parents we were engaged, my mother threw her hands over her head and exclaimed, "It's a miracle!" It was only the second time in my life I'd seen my father cry.

On January 5, 2002, Tim and I were married in my folks' living room. I started the adoption paperwork the day we returned from our honeymoon.

Chapter 3

THE BABY FROM TOTONICAPÁN

I discovered Yolanda Sánchez while sitting in my cubicle at the San Francisco Museum of Modern Art on a Monday morning in late May 2002. Her agency, Across the Border Adoptions, featured photo listings of Guatemalan infants so new to the world their eyes weren't yet opened. Fingernails as tiny as match heads, mouths the size of miniature rose petals. Their dark hair glistened flat against their heads, still wet from being born.

Stacks of glossy adoption brochures sat on our kitchen table, filled with pictures of "Russian princesses" and "China dolls," home at last with their "forever families." But it was Yolanda's website to which I was addicted. Every morning for a month I arrived at work an hour early, and before I had taken the lid off my coffee, I logged onto my computer to check the babies' status. "Emily with the enchanting eyes," "Darling Jacklyn," and "Healthy Hannah" were listed for only a week or two before a family claimed them. How could the adopting parents make a decision based on a photo? Wasn't the temptation to fall in love with the most adorable child—logic and health concerns forgotten? Yet here I was, scrolling through Yolanda's website, falling in love myself.

After returning from our honeymoon, I began assembling our adoption dossier, the required compendium of facts about us that I ultimately had notarized and authenticated by the Secretary of State in Sacramento: a home study compiled after three interviews with a licensed social worker; copies of birth, marriage, and divorce certificates; three personal reference letters and one from the California State Police Department verifying we had no criminal records; tax returns; medical reports; and, finally, fingerprint clearance from the Department of Homeland Security.

In adoption parlance, Tim and I were "paper-ready." We could have signed with any one of the agencies whose brochures sat on our kitchen table. The agency would have added our names to the bottom of the waiting list, and after two or three months, assigned us a child in a step called the "referral."

Or I could call Yolanda. She didn't "refer" us a baby; we asked for the one we wanted. Her babies were adoptable immediately, no waiting required. At least that was what she claimed on her website.

On a Wednesday afternoon in July, I entered an unused conference room and closed the door. I circled the conference table three times before Yolanda's answering machine picked up on the eleventh ring. The brisk outgoing message was in English, Spanish, and French.

"My name is Jessica O'Dwyer," I stammered after the beep. "My husband, Tim Berger, and I are considering adoption from Guatemala."

"Hello? *Soy* Yolanda. I'm here."

"I saw your website."

"You choose your baby," Yolanda purred. "We get paperwork done, quick."

"But we've only been married seven months. Every other agency says we need to be married two years."

"You don't need to be married at all! Look at me, I'm single myself. I adopted one girl already and am adopting a second."

"My husband is over fifty. I'm almost forty-four. They say we can't adopt an infant."

"As long as one parent is under fifty, you can adopt whoever you want."

"Even an infant?"

Yolanda laughed heartily, as though I had just told her the funniest joke.

"Jessica,"—she pronounced my name *Yessica*—"you want the baby or not?"

Maybe if Tim and I hadn't been so old—maybe if we'd found each other in our twenties instead of in mid-life after our divorces—I wouldn't have felt so much pressure to make a decision quickly.

"All my babies is in foster care," Yolanda murmured.

The private foster care system was the most compelling reason

Americans adopted from Guatemala. Instead of growing up in orphanages, the children lived in private homes, doted on by Guatemalan foster mothers. Costs were covered by the adoption fees paid by the American parents. This especially appealed to Tim as a physician. He was a dermatologist, not a pediatrician, but he appreciated how crucial dedicated early care was for an infant.

"Your baby can be home in six months," Yolanda said.

Every book and article we had read on the subject stated that the younger a baby was when she entered a permanent family situation, the easier her transition. Adopting an older child practically guaranteed future challenges. Two different social workers I had spoken with said Guatemala was the country they would adopt from themselves.

At first we had assumed we would adopt a Russian baby with blue eyes and light hair—a baby who looked like us—or a little Chinese girl who was abandoned because of her country's one-child policy. But children from those countries came home at ten months or older. Guatemalan adoption meant our child would look nothing like us, but her life might be easier because she joined our family at a younger age.

Guatemala made sense for another reason that was equally important to me. Chances were a baby born there would have been baptized Catholic if she stayed in her country of origin. My family was Irish Catholic. Religion was something we could share.

Almost as if she were reading my mind, Yolanda said, "We make sure your baby gets baptized before she gets on the plane."

That line from Yolanda prompted me to trust her more than anything else. A Catholic herself, she understood my need to know our daughter was baptized before we put her in harm's way on an airplane.

"Let me talk it over with my husband," I said, making a note to research the museum's family leave policy.

"Is easy," said Yolanda. "Six months will pass like a flash."

Yolanda gave me only one reference, a psychiatrist in Fresno who emailed me a photo of her five-year-old daughter, Graciela, along with a short letter. I opened the file alone at my desk early Thursday morning. Little Graciela was curtsying in a yellow ballet costume. "Daffodil" the caption read. Her black hair was shiny as a seal's coat.

I kept Graciela's image on my computer screen all morning, studying each pixel as though it had something magical to reveal, shrinking it to the toolbar any time a coworker approached. At the end of the day, after everyone else had gone, I printed the picture at the color printer and stared at it like a star-struck teenager.

"Look how adorable she is," I said to Tim that night when he arrived home after I'd finished dinner. On clinic nights, he always worked late. "And she came home at four months."

Tim skimmed the psychiatrist's letter, nodding at the words "healthy," "intelligent," and "active." According to the note, Graciela was on target for developmental milestones; moreover, she was extremely musical and promised to be gifted at ballet, too. The only challenge the psychiatrist had faced during the process involved communication with Yolanda, which she attributed to Yolanda's limited English skills. Yolanda was from Uruguay; her first language was Spanish. Graciela's mother advised that we stick to email. Other than that, she recommended Yolanda's services. Adopting their daughter was the single best thing she and her husband had ever done.

Seven pounds at birth was the magic number for Tim, the number which indicated a healthy baby who would flourish. Unlike most adoptive parents who preferred newborns, he preferred a baby slightly older because many serious potential health risks revealed themselves after the first month. Gender, he left to me. Because I grew up with three sisters, I chose a girl.

I continued reading the literature from other agencies and contacting their references. I even filled out a few applications and sent in deposits. But every morning it was Yolanda's website I logged onto, hopeful that my daughter would appear. And one day she did.

Her name was Stefany Mishell Xoc Toledo. Born May 20, 2002. Seven pounds at birth, she was two months old when her photo was posted. From my reading on Guatemalan culture, I knew the name "Xoc" was indigenous, indicating her birth mother was from one of the country's twenty-three native tribes. Stefany's straight black hair and dark brown skin confirmed this. She was so clearly annoyed at being photographed that her expression made me laugh out loud. In her eyes, I saw resolve and independence, a born survivor.

Right away I knew she was our daughter.

I told my boss I had a family emergency and raced down the stairs to catch the express bus to Tim's office across town. The bus ride took less than twenty minutes, but when it stopped at his corner, I was practically hyperventilating.

I dashed the two short blocks to the clinic and sprinted though the automatic doors to the elevator. Bypassing the front desk staff, I sneaked into the examining room area directly and intercepted Tim as he rushed out of one room toward another, his white coat flapping behind him. On clinic days, Tim never sat down. I called him the "hardest-working man in dermatology."

"I have to show you something," I said, pulling him across the hall into his office. I shut the door behind us.

"I only have five minutes," Tim said.

I stumbled over a ream of papers on the floor and sat in his desk chair.

Tim observed Stefany's picture, looking as detached as if he were still in an exam room. I knew that before he became emotionally invested, he would want to see birth records, doctor's reports, and Apgar scores that predicted the baby's ability to thrive. I sat in his desk chair while he set his phone to speaker, and together we called Yolanda.

We learned that the baby was healthy and big. Her birth mother,

Ana, was thirty-two years old. Ana was from the *altiplano* or highlands, a village called Totonicapán. Her husband was dead. She moved to Guatemala City to work as a housekeeper to support her two other children. She became pregnant with a much-younger man who had promised to marry her but abandoned her instead. Yolanda made a *tsk-tsk* sound.

"I fax you the birth certificate right now," Yolanda said.

Written in Spanish, the birth certificate stated that Stefany weighed six pounds ten ounces at birth, and not seven pounds as Yolanda claimed. She wasn't born in Guatemala City, either, but in Antigua, a town forty-five minutes north of the capital. However, a scrawled note from a Guatemalan pediatrician indicated a healthy checkup at two months. Stefany was gaining weight and was alert and responsive. No evidence of syphilis, hepatitis, or HIV.

We told Yolanda we needed to think over our decision. But that night we talked about airplane reservations and at what point we should visit. If we visited before the adoption was final, Stefany would enter the U.S. on an IR-3 visa, bestowing upon her automatic citizenship. If we didn't visit, she would enter on an IR-4 visa, necessitating an additional paperwork hoop.

We chose to visit; the sooner the better.

We tried to guess how tall Stefany would be and whether she'd be artistic or musical. We speculated on the ages of her siblings and if any of them had been adopted. Would she be intellectual like Tim or intuitive like me? Or a combination of us both?

Based on our feelings for Stefany and very little else, we decided to proceed with the adoption. In July 2002, we express-mailed Yolanda a certified check for $15,000, roughly three-fifths of her $25,000 fee. The balance was due when the adoption was completed, which by my initial calculation would be in January. Along with the check, I sent the completed Power of Attorney form that Yolanda had emailed us. Guatemalan adoptions were not handled by courts, but by private attorneys called *notarios*. By signing a Power of Attorney, we authorized a Guatemalan *notario* to act on our behalf.

We sent Stefany's picture to my parents, to Tim's mom, and to our combined six brothers and sisters. We painted the spare bedroom in a shade called Monet Haystack. My sister gave me the Spanish-language tapes her sons had outgrown. I signed up for once-a-week evening Spanish lessons at our local high school.

Yolanda sent us a contract that stated she was not liable should the adoption fall through. Things could happen that were beyond her control, and we shouldn't expect our money back. Maybe this should have signaled us to steer clear of Yolanda, but we signed the contract without any questions. To us, a contract connoted a business transaction, and we were trying to build a family. Not until we were months into the process did we realize that building a family through adoption *was* a business transaction—albeit one that involved the most precious commodity on earth—and by then we were too far in to do anything except keep going.

Chapter 4

LA FAMILIA GARZA

On November 1, Stefany was almost six months old, and we were no further along in the adoption process than we had been in July. We were stalled on step two, the DNA test. Guatemala was the only country from which the U.S. required DNA. The prerequisite was instituted in 1999, after allegations that women were posing as mothers of babies who weren't theirs. The DNA test proved a baby wasn't kidnapped. Samples were collected from mother and child and sent to a lab in North Carolina to verify they matched. The U.S. Embassy then issued its "pre-approval."

I sat in my museum cubicle and sent Yolanda the same email message I'd sent daily for the past two weeks: "DNA????????"

That afternoon, I received one of her standard excuses: "The teachers are on strike and the roads are closed." The day before, it was because the in-country facilitator, Theodore, had car trouble and the garage lacked the necessary part. The day before that, Ana missed the appointment. Or Theodore couldn't find her.

What was going on down there? Every other agency administered DNA within days of getting a signed Power of Attorney. A flow chart tacked up in my cubicle beside a montage of photos taken of Stefany at the Camino Real reminded me how far we still had to go:

* Power of Attorney registered in Guatemala

* DNA match and U.S. Embassy pre-approval

* Guatemala Family Court interviews Ana

* Case sent to Procuraduría General de la Nación (PGN) for review and approval

* New birth certificate and Guatemalan passport to travel

* Documents translated and submitted to U.S. Embassy for "pink slip"

* Medical exam by U.S. Embassy doctor

* U.S. Embassy interview with us and Stefany

* Home!

Only the first item was checked off. How would we ever be done by January?

The second week in November, Yolanda emailed that the DNA test had been administered, but the North Carolina lab had lost the results. "It happen sometimes," she wrote.

I sat at my desk and opened my mouth in a silent scream. After all the effort it took to get the DNA sample, how could someone lose it? Wouldn't very close tabs be kept on it? Still staring at my computer screen, I paged Tim with the "22222" code we used for emergencies. He rang back immediately.

"Are you kidding?" he said. "Every hospital in the country sends tissue samples to that lab everyday, and as far as I know they've never lost a single one."

"You think Yolanda's lying?" My voice was loud in the quiet office.

Tim backpedaled. Like me, he wanted to believe the best of Yolanda. He put down the phone and I heard him shuffling papers. He found the number for the lab and told me to call it myself.

"No ma'am," drawled the technician who answered the phone. "We have no record of receiving that sample. I wish I could say otherwise."

I held myself together long enough to say thank you.

Saturday afternoon I was in the kitchen loading the dishwasher when my parents called from San Diego.

"How you doing, kiddo?" My father's voice boomed over the speakerphone. He was a retired high school industrial arts teacher and still spoke loudly enough to be heard in the last row.

"Great." I rinsed a plate and slid it into the dishwasher's bottom rack.

"Where's my favorite dermatologist?" asked my mother, a former Radio City Music Hall Rockette who loved that I'd married a doctor.

I answered that Tim was in the garage, cleaning the bikes

after our long ride that morning. Forty-five miles. My father let out a long, low whistle.

"Once you get that baby, you won't be able to go on those long rides," my mother said.

Recently, she was quick to point out the ways our freedom would be curtailed once we became parents. I told her we'd hike instead.

"They can get a trailer thing," said my father.

"But those are so dangerous!"

"A seat in the back, then."

"And if they fall over?"

"They're not going to fall over."

As usual, my parents had launched into a discussion between themselves, forgetting my presence entirely. I loaded the glasses into the top shelf and closed the dishwasher as I waited for them to settle down.

"You don't have to worry about a bike trailer," I said. "Or a seat in the back. We've got bigger concerns."

I explained that adoption from Guatemala required a DNA match, and we didn't have one. Nothing would happen until we did. "By the time we resolve this, Stefany could be riding a two-wheeler."

"You're the Unsinkable Molly Brown," my father said.

"Maybe it's for the best," said my mother. "Maybe it's just not meant to be."

The door from the garage opened and Tim walked into the kitchen, his hands dirty from cleaning the bikes.

"Here's Tim." I thrust the phone into his dirty hand, mouthed the words "my parents," and stalked out of the kitchen.

Let Tim finish the conversation. Let him listen to the tale of my parents' friend's seven-year-old granddaughter who was adopted and didn't know how to tie her own shoelaces. Let him try to convince them that even though we'd never been pregnant, we felt like we were Stefany's real parents.

I adored my parents and knew they adored me. But they didn't understand that from the moment I had held Stefany in my arms, she became my daughter. That I felt destined to be her mother, and always would. Would my mother be so cavalier if she was at risk for losing one of her own children?

I was still fuming in the middle of the hallway when the buzzer on the dryer went off. I marched over to the laundry room and pulled out an armload of warm towels.

I wanted Stefany home with us.

I turned toward the end of hallway and stood outside the door to her yellow bedroom.

It was the perfect space for a baby girl. White cotton curtains with gingham pullbacks. A curlicue headboard on a wooden crib. A shelf full of board books sent by my sisters: *Owl Babies, Runaway Bunny, The Very Hungry Caterpillar*. An antique rocking chair I'd refinished in high school. And on the white dresser, three framed photographs from our visit with Stefany.

The one in the middle was my favorite. Stefany was asleep in my arms, her head resting on my shoulder. She was so rarely relaxed during the three days we spent together, I asked Tim to take a picture so I wouldn't forget the moment. I was surprised at how heavy her head was, how warm her small body.

I sat in the rocker and pushed myself back gently, the warm towels pressed against my heart.

Unlike other countries, Guatemala allowed adopting parents to visit their children as often as they liked until the adoption was final and to keep the baby with them in their hotel room. For most Americans at the Camino Real, this equaled one or two weekend visits before the final pickup, which usually occurred within six months of starting the process. Our number of visits was limited only by our accrued vacation days at work. We planned to visit as often as possible.

The only proviso was that virtually every adoption agency forbade any visits until the DNA matched and the Embassy issued its pre-approval because without DNA and Embassy pre-approval, there would be no adoption. No point in a family bonding with a child they couldn't have.

Not so with Yolanda. When I informed her we planned to visit Stefany for a second time over the Thanksgiving weekend, she didn't object. "Bring more diapers. Vitamins. Formula," she emailed. "Diaper rash cream!"

We arrived at Aurora International Airport at seven o'clock on Thanksgiving morning and fell in behind the crowd of returning nationals, most of them shorter than we were and nearly every one carrying a microwave, toaster, iron, or other boxed appliance. Once again, our bags were so stuffed with supplies for Stefany it took both of us to haul them off the luggage carousel.

At that early hour, the capital city looked like a ghost town. Aluminum shades were drawn tightly over shop windows, steel gates were padlocked across front doors. Two uniformed guards carrying machine guns stood in the driveway of a Volkswagen dealership. We passed a Domino's Pizza and a Chuck E. Cheese, both locked down.

Guatemala was still recovering from a bloody civil war that had raged between the military government and the indigenous Maya population for thirty-six years. When the conflict ended in 1996, an estimated two hundred thousand Maya were dead. A United Nations truth commission blamed government-backed forces for the majority of the murders. On our first trip, the number of soldiers with weapons had shocked me. This time I expected it, but was nonetheless unsettled by the sight of so many fingers on so many triggers.

Our taxi rounded a traffic circle and merged onto the wide boulevard of Avenida Reforma. Tall shade trees dotted the avenue's center island, but the grass was sparse and patchy. We passed a block-long *típica* market that sold textiles and paintings. The driver made a sharp right into the arcing driveway of the Camino

Real. A tiny woman in a brightly embroidered blouse, called a *huipil*, waved as we passed. She held up a rag doll wearing a colorful costume and thick black braids. Two girls stood beside her, almost miniature size.

Before we came to a full stop, two bellmen sprinted out from the lobby. One opened our taxi door while a second opened the trunk for our luggage. Tim peeled off a dollar for each of them and paid the cab driver with a ten-dollar bill. Our bank was unable to convert dollars to the local currency, the *quetzal*, but everyone seemed happy with dollars. Tim waited with the bellmen while I ran down the driveway to the woman and girls.

"How much?" I pointed to the doll.

"*Veinte quetzales.*" About three dollars.

I dug out a five-dollar bill from my purse. The doll would be a memento for Stefany, a reminder of how we had met at the hotel. The woman pressed the bill against her leg to flatten it before tucking it into her apron pocket with her child-sized fingers. She stared at me with hard eyes. I smiled at the girls, but they were already scouting for other customers.

I was glad to be back at the Camino Real. "We met you on that sofa," I imagined telling Stefany. "I recognized you from across the room." When we checked in, the reception clerk said he'd put us on the ninth floor. "The adoption floor," he said, swiping our credit card through his machine.

"Do you think he remembers us?" I asked Tim as the elevator doors swished shut and we were whisked toward our room.

"Us, or people like us," Tim said.

Stefany didn't know who I was. When Lupe tried to hand her to me in the hotel lobby, Stefany tucked her head into Lupe's neck and hid her face.

I threw back my shoulders and stood tall. Arranged my face in a pleasant expression. Kept my voice upbeat. It wasn't her fault. The situation was to blame. She was six months old.

During our September visit, she had barely drunk from her bottle. At night, she screamed for six hours straight. But by Sunday afternoon, she'd been comfortable enough to sip formula while gazing into my eyes. Afterward was the memorable moment when she fell asleep, her head against my shoulder. And then it was time to return her to Lupe.

Now here we were again, two months later. Strangers.

The adoption books said it was good that she was bonded to someone because that attachment would be transferred to us. Any bond was better than none.

Attachment took time. We were only visiting for a long weekend.

Patience, patience, patience.

I had ridden my bicycle across the Anza-Borrego Desert. I could do this.

Before Lupe left the Camino Real, she invited us to come for dinner the following night at her home for a typical *chapín* meal: *carne asada*, black bean paste, white cheese, and plantains. *Chapín* was a slang name for people from Guatemala, used by Guatemalans and other peoples in Central America. The term referred to the traditional hand-hewn leather sandals worn by the ancient Maya.

Yolanda had said we shouldn't leave the hotel except to buy diapers or bottled water from the market around the corner, or to run to the pharmacy next door for medicine. But the chance to see Stefany in her familiar home environment was too tempting to pass up.

At 5:00 PM, the Garzas' maroon Camry sedan pulled in front of the Camino Real, where Tim and I waited with Stefany. The front passenger door swung open, and a pink blanket fell to the pavement as Lupe scrambled out. She grabbed Stefany from me as though they'd been separated much longer than twenty-four hours. Stefany reached her hand up to her foster mother's face as if to convince herself that Lupe was real. The greeting was so different from the one I'd received that I had to turn away.

Lupe's husband, Francisco, turned off the ignition and walked around from the driver's side. His black wavy hair was brushed back from his high forehead. His hips were as narrow as a samba dancer's. One gold front tooth flashed as he shook Tim's hand.

The Camry had shoulder harnesses, but no baby seat. I tamped down visions of a shattered windshield as Lupe arranged the fallen pink blanket across her lap and set Stefany on it.

Tim and I clambered into the back seat to find Lupe's daughter, Vivian, squeezed into the driver-side corner. Unlike her mother, who was broad-shouldered and square, Vivian was reed slender. Her black hair was pulled back in a tight bun. After surprising us with an easy "Hello, how are you," she told us she used English regularly in her job as a receptionist for the Guatemalan tourist bureau, *Inguat*. Francisco also worked for *Inguat*, but spoke only enough English to claim he didn't speak any. He led tour groups from Italy and was fluent in Italian.

Lupe spoke the language of babies. That secret, special language was her native tongue. As the car sat stalled in rush hour traffic, I observed Lupe in the front seat, chattering with Stefany. Stefany's body softened; she melted into Lupe. Lupe wrapped her in the pink blanket, as snug as a papoose. Stefany's head dropped against Lupe's shoulder. I pressed my hands against my chest and imagined her weight against me.

Francisco reached across the front seat and tousled Stefany's hair. "*Mi morenita*," he said. "My little dark brown one."

He often described people in terms of their skin color. He and Lupe were *café* or light brown. Vivian was *blanquita*. Tim and I were *gringos*, generic white people from anywhere north of Mexico.

The Garzas were what Guatemalans called *Ladino*, descended from European Hispanics, primarily, and the Germans who arrived at the turn of the century to begin many of the country's coffee plantations. Stefany was *indígena* or Maya, terms that replaced

Indian following the 1996 peace accord. It felt strange to be among people who discussed skin color so openly and at such length. In the States, such observations were impolite. In Guatemala, they were normal conversation.

Tim asked a question about the layout of Guatemala City. Vivian explained that the capital was divided into zones, which Tim compared to zip codes in the United States. Downtown was Zone 1; the airport was Zone 13; and the Camino Real was in Zone 10, known as the *Zona Viva*.

"Where are we going?" Tim asked.

Zone 21, on the farthest outskirts of the city. At last, the city fell away behind us and we entered a less-developed, suburban area spotted with a series of gated communities that I knew were middle-class, but looked more like maximum-security prisons. Francisco approached one, indistinguishable from the others except for a stand of scrubby young pine trees. A guard at the entrance waved us in, and we drove toward a quad of squat cinderblock buildings with iron bars on every window. The courtyard was empty.

Behind one of the buildings, we parked on a dirt lot so rutted my ankle twisted when I stepped out of the car. Lupe climbed out of the front seat with Stefany. The women fell behind Francisco and Tim as though they were protecting us.

The front door of the Garzas' second-floor apartment was solid steel, with a small sliding window at the top to communicate with visitors. On the cement walkway out front, their eldest son, Victor, grilled thin strips of beef in a car tire rim filled with smoldering coals. Stefany squealed when she saw him, the happy recognition of a baby sister for her big brother. He swept her from Lupe's arms, called her *Mishellita*, and bench-pressed her over his head four times before returning her to Lupe.

A small table with eight mismatched chairs, set for dinner, took up half the living room, which smelled like sautéed onions.

Lupe handed Stefany to Vivian and walked through a set of swinging doors into the kitchen. Vivian's younger sisters—Maribel, a skinny sixteen-year-old in Dr. Martens combat boots and heavy black eyeliner, and Claudia, a shy preteen in a soccer uniform—sat on a sofa watching Spanish MTV. When Vivian introduced us, they mumbled their greetings. Claudia reached for Stefany with eager hands. Tim and I watched, astounded, as Stefany bounced her head to the beat.

"No wonder she's so bored with us in the hotel room," I said to Tim. "We're playing peek-a-boo and she's used to watching Shakira."

Tim and I were not sure what to do next. Stefany didn't need us. There was nowhere to sit down. The only light came from the TV set. The cinderblock walls were unadorned: no pictures or family photographs or framed diplomas for us to look at or pretend to look at.

There was no baby paraphernalia, the stuff I saw at my sisters' houses: baskets of toys, educational mobiles, building blocks in primary colors. The single piece of baby equipment was an ExerSaucer, the one piece of gear that I had read was dangerous and detrimental to a baby's ability to learn to walk. Yolanda had said that Guatemalan babies didn't crawl. As I looked around at the cramped space, I wondered if it was because they had nowhere to go.

Lupe rushed in from the kitchen in a butcher's apron, balancing plates of beans and plantains on her forearms. She rushed back for a basket of tortillas and a liter-size bottle of Coke. Victor placed a plate of steaming meat in the middle of the table. The girls turned off the television and brought in Stefany. When the baby reached for Vivian instead of me, I pretended to be checking on the bags of gifts we brought that I had set by the front door.

Lupe untied her apron and sat at the end of the table closest to the swinging doors. Vivian set the baby on Lupe's lap. I sat next to Lupe and wiggled my finger for Stefany to latch onto, but she was more interested in the basket of tortillas. When I pushed the basket toward her, Lupe intercepted it, plucked out a tortilla, and folded it in half to give Stefany a nibble. I longed to ask Lupe if I could hold Stefany, but Lupe had Stefany lodged under her arm in a proprietary way.

Tim nudged my thigh with his, a reminder that I needed to rise above whatever I was feeling and make the most of this experience. Stefany was happy. That's what was important.

The beef was stringy and tough, but very flavorful. The tortillas were handmade. Tim was the cook in our family, and he asked Lupe how she prepared her *chirmol,* a tomato and onion salad that Lupe served with the beef. The secret ingredient, she said, was hot green chilies. Francisco apologized for the lukewarm Coke, explaining that the Garzas didn't drink tap water or use ice. We told him it didn't matter. They had invited us to their home and served a special meal. We were honored.

We gave the family as much as we could. Not only baby clothes, diapers, and formula for Stefany, but clothes and accessories for their family, too. When we visited the first time in September, we had given the Garzas drawing tablets and packs of colored pencils, like Yolanda recommended. This trip, however, I had brought what they really wanted: designer handbags, logo jackets, blue jeans, and baseball caps—articles that broadcast "U.S.A."

For dessert, Lupe set a plate of *canillas de leche*, a milk-fudge flavored with cinnamon, between Tim and me. Like many Guatemalan desserts, the dish was extremely simple but intensely sweet. One *canilla*, or finger, was enough to satisfy any craving for sugar.

I asked what we should bring down the next time we visited.

"*Zapatos*," Lupe said, and everyone gave me their shoe sizes.

"English-language tapes," said Victor.

"Makeup, T-shirts, Xbox." Vivian translated for the girls as I wrote down colors and styles.

Francisco said, "A new car."

"You mean like, driving?" Tim pantomimed sitting behind a steering wheel.

"*Sí*," Francisco confirmed, as casually as he'd specified his shoe size.

Tim spread his arms wide. "A car is very big. Too big for an airplane."

To the foster family, we were rich Americans so nothing was impossible. We stayed at the most expensive hotel in Guatemala City and flew regularly on airplanes. Tim was a doctor and I worked at a museum. We both graduated from college. We were adopting a baby, which they knew was a very expensive proposition.

After the dishes had been cleared, Tim and I were treated to what we later referred to as our daughter's "repertoire." If we prompted Stefany with the word *besitos*, she threw us a kiss; if we said *aplaude*, enthusiastic hand-clapping ensued. The word *ojitos* translated to "little eyes," and when Stefany heard it, she was transformed into an eye-batting coquette. *Adiós* provoked a hand-wave backwards, the Guatemalan *bye-bye* equivalent.

Stefany's performance was so charming and cute, I simply had to hold her. But when I reached for her, she let out a loud scream and clawed her way back to Lupe. I sank back to my chair, devastated.

Stefany didn't want me. As far as she was concerned, Lupe was her mother. "Barren" was not a word I'd ever used to describe myself, but barren was how I felt.

Chapter 5

NIKKI

∿∿∿∿∿∿∿∿∿∿∿∿∿∿∿∿∿∿∿∿∿∿∿

January 3, 2003. Six months after we'd signed our Power of Attorney, our case was in the same state it had been in November: No DNA or Embassy pre-approval. Yolanda blamed Theodore. Theodore blamed Yolanda. They both blamed Guatemala, which Yolanda referred to as "the Congo." Tim and I were concerned, but not yet worried. Pregnancy took nine months. Maybe we were in the gestation period.

It was the weekend of our first wedding anniversary and Tim had asked me how I wanted to celebrate. A bike ride around Lake Tahoe? Hike in Yosemite? How about wine-tasting in Napa or a drive to Mendocino? We had enjoyed each of those activities before we started the adoption.

"Visit our daughter," I said, as if he had to ask. Most newlyweds spent their first year as an uninterrupted love-fest. Tim and I had spent the past twelve months filling out paperwork and planning trips to Guatemala.

The Camino Real's ninth floor was full when we checked in for our third three-day visit. By mid-morning Saturday, the temperature had reached seventy-eight degrees. We slathered on sunscreen and headed with Stefany to the hotel pool. The pool was long enough for lap swimming, with a mosaic bottom of gorgeous Mediterranean blue. We heard tennis balls being thwacked somewhere on the hotel grounds. The sky was clear and aromatic with eucalyptus leaves.

One side of the pool deck was occupied by Guatemalan families who held memberships to the hotel's health club. The children played Marco Polo while their mothers, dressed in sarongs and high heels, sipped espresso delivered to their lounge chairs by waiters in starched white shirts and bow ties. To be elite in Guatemala was to belong to a very small subset; in a country of some thirteen million people, the top twenty percent of the population controlled two-thirds of the income. Almost everybody else eked out a living by subsistence farming and seasonal farmwork.

The other side of the pool deck was occupied by Americans. Dressed in tankinis and flip-flops, the mothers sat on their lounge chairs playing patty-cake with their Guatemalan babies while the fathers circled, video-cameras whirring.

"We're going to check out the shallow end," Tim said, taking Stefany from me. "Why don't you take a nap?"

The night before, I had paced the ninth-floor hall with Stefany, logging what felt like miles. Nothing I did calmed her. I wasn't alone, either. Over the course of five hours, I met four other parents padding down the hallway. I understood why the hotel staff put the adoptive families on one floor.

I settled into a lounge chair in the American section of the pool deck. A deeply tanned woman with a streaked blonde ponytail and designer sunglasses wheeled up a stroller piled with white hotel towels. She frowned as she shielded her eyes to gauge the position of the sun. Her husband carried a Guatemalan toddler on his shoulders.

"Would you mind sharing your umbrella?" she asked.

"Of course not," I said. "I've seen you around the hotel. I'm Jessica."

"Nikki." She unloaded the towels from the stroller and arranged one lengthwise for her body and another for her back.

She stretched out and pulled a *People* magazine from a tote bag, opening it across her knees. She had a French tip pedicure and a gold toe ring. A gigantic, four-carat diamond solitaire the size of a small doorknob glistened on her left finger. She smelled like expensive perfume.

We both watched Nikki's husband and toddler son splash in the shallow end. Tim was there, too, coaxing Stefany to let go of his neck. Stefany was terrified of water. Even when Tim tried to bathe her in the hotel sink she arched her back and screamed. Each time, I couldn't bear it and covered my eyes.

"Your daughter's cute," Nikki said. "How old is she?"

This was always the first question. "Eight months. How old's your son?"

"Fourteen months."

I nodded. Six months older than Stefany probably meant Nikki had been waiting for him half a year longer than I had. The unwritten rule among adoptive parents was that those with younger children shouldn't gloat in front of those whose children were older. Every minute seemed like an eternity when you were waiting for your child. Nobody needed to be reminded of that.

I waved to Stefany and called, "Don't be scared, sweetheart."

"What agency are you using?" Nikki asked.

This was always the second question. "It's a facilitator, actually. Her name's Yolanda."

Nikki shook her head so hard her sunglasses slipped halfway down her face. She grabbed them from her nose and folded them onto the table beside her. "Yolanda Sánchez?"

"You've heard of her?"

Nikki lifted the magazine from her knees and dropped it to the ground. "Let me tell you something. If there was a way for my husband to put that woman out of business forever and get away with it, he would. You understand what I'm talking about?" A deep furrow appeared on her forehead. "We didn't even know who Yolanda *was*. When we couldn't get pregnant, we hired an adoption attorney in New Jersey, which is where we're from. We went through the domestic stuff, and twice the birth mother changed her mind on us at the last minute. Once, she was in the hospital on the delivery table. So we told the attorney, 'Find us someone somewhere who's not going to change her mind.' We didn't know anything about Guatemala. But we're Italian and dark, so we said 'Why not?' Next thing you know, we get pictures of this darling little boy. One thing leads to another and we learn that there's this woman involved, a facilitator from Los Angeles named Yolanda."

Nikki looked around and lowered her voice to a whisper. "You know how it works here, right? The birth mother signs the baby over to a Guatemalan attorney, which they call a *notario*. They're like a package. It's not like in China where they drop the baby on a doorstep and that's the end. They make the birth mother sign her permission four different times. It's a lot of work because half the mothers live in the middle of nowhere and the *notario* can't find them. If you have a shit *notario* who's lazy, excuse my language, you're screwed."

"You have a choice?"

"If you're smart you do. Some people sign with an agency specifically for the *notario*. But the only kind Yolanda uses are shit *notarios* because they're the cheapest." Nikki shuddered. "Yolanda's shrewd. Her father owned a very successful export company in Uruguay. Yolanda saw how easy it is to move property between two countries, as long as you do it in the space where no one is watching. Corners can easily be cut."

A waiter in a starched shirt and bow tie stood in front of us with an order pad. "Diet Coca-Cola?" he asked Nikki.

"Two please," said Nikki. "I'll get this," she said as I reached for my purse. "They know me here. Charge to my *cuarto, por favor.*"

Nikki paused, squinting out at the other side of the pool. "You think the Guatemalans over there care about a bunch of Mayan Indian kids they wouldn't adopt themselves? They adopt from Ukraine, for Christ's sake. They want white-skinned babies."

She leaned down to pick up her magazine and dropped it into her tote bag. "The *notarios* are worse. They're only in it for the money."

I did not expect this conversation. Most parents we met knew as little about the process as we did. But I grew up in New Jersey around people like Nikki: outspoken folks who called it as they saw it. In New Jersey, you didn't have to wonder what people were thinking or how they felt because they told you.

I moved closer to her lounge chair. "Yolanda said that Stefany's birth mother walked into the hotel, pregnant, looking for Yolanda. Do you think that's possible?" As soon as I said this out loud I felt foolish. There was no way that an indigenous woman in full *traje*—embroidered *huipil* and hand-woven skirt—would be allowed to set foot in the lobby of the Camino Real.

"Rich adoption people don't socialize with poor pregnant girls from the highlands," Nikki said. "They've got a network all over the country. They're called *buscadoras*. It's like the word in Spanish, *buscar,* 'to look for.' They're intermediaries. If a girl gets pregnant, what's she supposed to do? So her aunt or her neighbor or a friend... someone knows someone who knows the *buscadora,* who contacts the *notario* to draw up the papers."

Nikki's explanation sounded plausible. In a country that lacked social services, welfare, or food stamps—not to mention access to birth control or legal abortion—it made sense that an informal network of women had developed to help pregnant women place their babies. Most likely, a *buscadora* had connected Ana with Yolanda.

"Yolanda stopped paying my *notario,*" Nikki said. "And she claimed to do things she never did."

"We don't have DNA," I said.

"Typical. One of the bellboys told me he knows where Theodore lives. Theodore, who's supposed to help us while we're here, right? Inside his house, floor to ceiling, are boxes and boxes of stuff these trusting Americans send down, which the baby never sees. And I want to scream, 'Wake up people! Those diapers, that formula you think your babies are getting? Guess what? They're not.'"

Nikki pressed her manicured hands against each of her temples and massaged slowly, the sun glinting off her diamond. "Yolanda told us to send a picture, you know? We sent a picture, and I'm thinking my son is sleeping with it every night in his crib. When I got here the foster family had no idea who I was. No idea about a picture. I kept saying 'Didn't you get our picture?' They looked at me like I was a lunatic."

Nikki's voice broke off. The waiter placed two Diet Cokes on napkins on the small table between us.

Nikki signed the bill. "*Gracias*," she said.

"In October, he had a lump on his forehead right over his eye." Nikki cupped her hand to her face to show me where the lump was. "Don't get me wrong, his foster mother is great. We're like family. But when I saw that black eye, I told my husband either I move to Guatemala to take care of my son or you find yourself another wife." She reached for her soda. "That was ten weeks ago."

"You've been in the hotel the whole time?" I asked.

She nodded. "It's okay. My son's fine now and my husband's racked up a ton of frequent flyer miles."

I picked up my Coke and took a sip as I studied Nikki from behind my sunglasses. Her appearance was misleading: Like other scrappy New Jersey natives, Nikki had the heart of a prize fighter. She kept standing. She didn't back down. Our conversation made me realize that if Stefany was to become our daughter, I needed to be less passive in the process. Like Nikki, I had to put on my boxing gloves and climb into the ring. This was a lesson I would learn again and again during the next year. I must be prepared to fight.

We sat in our lounge chairs, two mothers watching their children frolic with their fathers in a swimming pool in Guatemala. Stefany was becoming a little more confident. She felt sure enough to release her arms from around Tim's neck and relax her shoulders into the water as he swirled her in a circle around him. Tim was in the center of the circle and he supported her securely, holding her under her arms so she would feel safe enough to trust him, and learn to be brave.

Chapter 6

YOLANDA

When we returned to San Francisco two days later, I called and emailed Yolanda so persistently she finally agreed we could come to her home office. The next Saturday, Tim and I were on the 405 freeway, driving south toward Los Angeles.

"Please don't talk to her about money," I reminded Tim as he slowed to look for Yolanda's house number at the end of a well-maintained cul-de-sac. Tim had done the math, and if Yolanda was processing 140 adoptions a year, as she claimed, she collected more than three million dollars annually. "We didn't come here to fight."

Tim pulled up in front of a rambling two-story ranch house painted the color of desert sand. The front door was painted fire-engine red; the lawn was clipped and green as Astroturf. Three oval rocks, carved with the words "Breathe," "Serenity," and "Bliss," were set at precise intervals in front of a sculptured jasmine bush whose sweet fragrance filled the late afternoon air.

"Definitely upscale," I said. "You're right about that."

We approached the front door holding hands and rang the bell. Then I noticed the mailbox. So many express-mail envelopes were stuffed inside that the box couldn't close. Each one, I was sure, contained the dossier of a family just like us. Jammed in together like that, one of them might easily get lost.

Yolanda looked older and more haggard in person than she did on her website. Her skin was mottled and lined. She shook Tim's hand first, after which she clasped the ends of my fingers, squeezing the tips. She looked me up and down, taking in my black jeans and ballet flats, and gave a disapproving sniff. In her navy blue dress with princess seams, Yolanda could have been dressed for a ladies' tea.

Yolanda's eyes shifted to that overflowing mailbox, then back to us. She stepped aside, without taking any of the mail, to let us in. Inside the entrance hall, she gestured to a rack by the door and asked that we remove our shoes. Her own sling-back sandals she left on. Their delicate, tapered heels sank into the off-white shag carpet as we followed her to the living room.

"Here in the dining room is my home office," she said and kept walking into the living room.

I gasped. Every inch of the dining room table was covered with piles of papers and more unopened express-mail envelopes. Stacks of birth certificates, marriage licenses, and passport copies were spread around on the floor, as if a two-year-old boy had thrown fists full of the documents into the air and scuffed them under his shoes when they landed. Gold foil seals of the secretaries of the states of California, Kansas, Texas, and Massachusetts gleamed on official papers that were wrinkled and torn, some under coffee cups half-filled with dregs of coffee. A film of gray grime coated the computer screen. The light on the telephone answering machine blinked "19" for the number of messages. I tugged the edge of Tim's sleeve, but he shook his head in a way that I knew meant, "Don't say anything."

We entered the living room, which was as baroque as the home's exterior was understated. Patterned gold wallpaper, oil paintings in heavy gilt-painted frames, and overstuffed furniture in textured white-on-white velvet. A towering Christmas tree, decorated top to bottom in glittery gold bows and a foot-high blinking star.

Tim and I sank into a velvet sofa so deep our knees were level with our eyes. Yolanda alighted on the edge of a white suede ottoman.

Tim seemed as collected as ever and engaged in small talk, but I couldn't stop thinking about that dining room table. I stared straight ahead at the Christmas tree, my hands balled into fists on my thighs.

"Stefany will be one in May," Tim said. "How much longer do you think it will take?"

I turned back toward Yolanda just in time to see a look of annoyance cross her face. "We can never say, Doctor. We cannot predict."

A young woman brought a tray of three glasses of sparkling water with crescents of lemon hooked over their rims. She handed a drink to Yolanda and waited while Yolanda gulped down the liquid, holding her hand to her throat as though coaxing down a large pill. Only then did the woman offer drinks to Tim and me. She backed out of the room without saying a word.

Yolanda's older daughter skipped in dressed in pink capris and a matching cotton sweater. I recognized her from Yolanda's website and knew she was adopted from Guatemala.

"This is Bianca." Yolanda encircled Bianca's slender wrist with her fingers and made a kissing sound at Bianca's forehead. "She's my first girl, adopted, eight years old."

Bianca had a heart-shaped face and a tumble of black curls. She looked nothing like Stefany, yet I longed to reach and touch her simply because she was from Guatemala.

Tim sat farther forward in the sofa and clasped his hands in a doctorly gesture meant to put her at ease. "What do you like to do after school?"

"I take riding lessons. And tennis at the country club."

Of all the sports she might have participated in, she had to mention the two most expensive. At the country club, no less. Yolanda may not have been processing families' dossiers, but she was definitely cashing their checks. I pressed my foot against Tim's.

Yolanda stood up abruptly. "Come, I show you the nursery."

We left our glasses and followed Yolanda up the stairs into a large, empty bedroom, painted pink. "We're still waiting for my second daughter, Pilar. Her adoption isn't final yet." She unfolded the accordion doors to the closet that covered the length of one wall. "See, I have clothes for all her ages."

From left to right, tiny triangle hangers held baby clothes for six months, nine months, one year, eighteen months, two toddler, three T, four. The clothes at the far end of the closet hung down almost twice as low as the clothes at the close end. On the floor of the closet were stacked bins, each one with a computer-generated label: onesies, pajamas, shoes, leggings.

"How old was Pilar when you started her adoption?" I asked.

"Six months." Yolanda reached for a hanger and fingered a tiny sleeper with prancing lambs around the collar.

"She seems pretty big now."

"She turned four last month."

A wave of heat shot through my body. "Is that normal?"

"Four years normal?" Yolanda frowned as if I should know better. "No. We got stuck."

Yolanda brushed past me and Tim and into the hallway. "She's in a very nice orphanage."

The top of my head felt as if it could blow off. Orphanage? Yolanda lived in a house like this and wouldn't pay for foster care? I was filled with anger on behalf of Pilar.

"What's taking so long?" I dug my fingernails into Tim's forearm. "What is she doing?"

Tim took off his glasses and wiped them on his shirt. "She isn't doing anything," he said.

Chapter 7

THE HAGUE

In March 2003, the rules of adoption changed. As of March 5, Guatemala was to abide by the provisions of the Hague Convention on Intercountry Adoption. "The Hague," as it was called in the adoption community, would abolish the long-standing notarial adoption system. Instead, a Central Authority would oversee the process. Going forward, any American agency that adopted from Guatemala must be certified as Hague-compliant. Yolanda's agency was not.

March 5 became the only date that mattered. If your Power of Attorney had been signed, translated, and filed in Guatemala before March 5, 2003, your adoption fell under the old rules. If your Power of Attorney was filed after that date, your adoption was suspended indefinitely, until the new system was set in place. Nobody knew when that would be.

We had signed our Power of Attorney eight months before, in July 2002. Yolanda had assured me it was filed, but after seeing her home office, and hearing about her from Nikki, we had serious doubts. But we couldn't lose faith in Yolanda because Stefany had been relinquished to Yolanda's *notario*. They were, as Nikki had said, a package. If we wanted Stefany, we had to deal with Yolanda.

Yolanda was incensed with the new system. While the country had been rapid to throw out the old system, it was much slower to institute a new one. Parents were reluctant to begin adoptions. "Nobody is doing nothing there," she wrote. "I have to return the babies on my website that nobody picked."

The Guatemalan *notarios* were up in arms. They lodged a formal complaint with the sitting Guatemalan president, Alfonso Portillo. The millions of dollars the *notarios* currently earned would instead be funneled through the Central Authority. The *notarios* would be out of business. They argued that the deadline was arbitrary, imposed before the new system was up and running. The Guatemalan government had acted prematurely.

No one, however, was more upset than adoptive parents. Children were in limbo. Lives were on hold. I looked up the website for the international watch-dog organization, Transparency International, to check their annual "Corruption Perception Index." Guatemala was ranked at number one hundred out of a possible one hundred thirty-three. Corruption-wise, that placed Guatemala a few notches below Thailand, Russia, Romania, and Ethiopia; and slightly above Sudan and Zimbabwe. Bribery and extortion were described as commonplace. Despite the Hague's best intentions, this information didn't inspire much confidence in the country's ability to install an adoption system that was better and more transparent than the existing one.

I felt sure that because we signed our Power of Attorney in July 2002, our adoption was grandfathered in. But I also knew that without a valid DNA test, we didn't have a case at all. Dozens of times a day, I checked the U.S. State Department website for updates. I corresponded with other clients of Yolanda in the same situation, every one of whom was as panicked as I was. Some sent prayer chain letters. Others threatened to complain to the Embassy. No one wanted to upset Yolanda, for fear of what she might do.

With two days to go before the new rules took effect, I was so distracted at work, I could hardly think. Instead of writing the press releases I had been assigned, I sat in front of my computer and stared at digital images of Stefany from our Christmas visit. When I got home, I drank a glass of red wine and ate popcorn for dinner. I organized every box in the pantry according to size and color, and spray-cleaned the stainless steel fronts to the refrigerator, dishwasher, and double-decker oven. With energy to burn, I got down on my hands and knees and scrubbed the kitchen floor.

When I heard the garage door open, signaling that Tim was home, I threw down my sponge and flung open the kitchen door. "It's March third!" I screamed. "We don't even know if our adoption has been filed."

Tim slipped past me, took his cell phone from his belt and placed it on the kitchen counter. "The clinic was incredibly busy today," he said with tired eyes. "Can I at least take off my shoes?"

"The clinic was *busy*?" I backed off dramatically, as if I might faint. "You think I *care*?"

Tim appeared stunned. He wasn't used to seeing me behave so sarcastically. We'd always treated each other with respect.

He padded over to the desk and flipped open the Rolodex. "Give me Yolanda's number," he said. He stuck out his palm, expecting it.

I ran over to the desk, alarmed. "What are you going to do?"

I spread my hands over the Rolodex, but he wrested out her information card and picked up the phone.

"Her machine." He looked past me as he spoke. "Hello Yolanda, this is Tim Berger up in Marin County. How are you?" He was using his socially polite voice. "I understand you're doing the best you can with the DNA. However, I'm calling to let you know that our lives have become a living hell"—he raised his hand to stop my protest—"a *living hell* because of it. Please call me as soon as possible so we can discuss our next steps. Thank you."

He clicked off the phone and replaced it in the receiver.

I leaned against the counter and glared at him. "She's not going to like that."

"I don't care," said Tim. "We can't live like this." He pulled another wine glass from the cabinet and filled it. "Cheers."

When Yolanda finally called back, Tim and I bolted up in bed from a deep sleep. The clock glowed "2:15."

Tim shook my leg, then pointed to the kitchen for me to go there and listen on the extension. I grabbed my robe, pulled it on, and groped my way from the bedroom to the kitchen. The phone was only halfway to my ear when I heard Yolanda yelling, "You think your life is hell? You don't know what is hell! Hell is when I walk into my office in Guatemala and there are three men with guns to my head so I pay the foster mothers. Or when I go to the villages to find the mothers, and the boyfriends and husbands of them is asking for money or food. Asking for medical services. Asking to pay the school. Asking to pay the funeral. Hell is when the biological mother tell me that her parents discover she is giving up the baby and they are after her. My own daughter fenced in miserable orphanage for four years. That is hell. I guarantee you will get a baby. I never guarantee nine months of joy. If you don't like the way I do business, I give the baby to someone else!"

Silence.

Dial tone.

I didn't remember dropping the phone, but I must have, because the battery flew out and skidded across the floor. Dizzy with fury, I ran back to our bedroom where Tim sat on the edge of the bed, the phone still in his hand.

"I told you not to call her! Now what? She takes the baby away? We could lose Stefany!"

I pushed him with such force that he almost fell backwards. I reached out to push him again and he grabbed my wrists.

"Why should she help us?" I shrieked. "She can't even help herself!"

"Listen to me." He put one hand on each of my cheeks and held my face. "I had the audacity to question Yolanda, and she's making me pay. But if you think this means we're walking away from our daughter, you're as crazy as she is."

Ten days passed before I called Yolanda again, groveling with an apology. I had no choice. Without her, we couldn't have Stefany. Yolanda laughed and told me that before she spoke to Tim the next time, she'd be sure to take her Valium.

The DNA samples from both Ana and Stefany were finally collected on March 25, 2003 and sent to the lab in North Carolina. We paid by credit card. A week later I received a statement from the lab in the mail that the match was 99.9 percent accurate. That indeed, this mother had given birth to this child. And there on the page for identification purposes were two clear copies of a photo of Ana holding Stefany on her lap.

No one could have doubted they were mother and child. Sadness flooded over me as I studied their similarities: the high, sharp cheekbones; the slightly upturned angle of their eyes; the intense blackness of their hair; their dark skin. Even their expressions were the same. I saw in Ana the woman I imagined Stefany would one day become: intelligent, noble, strong.

I stood at our kitchen counter, unable to move or sit down, with the lab report in front of me. In the first photograph, Ana leaned away from her baby, as though she were holding a stranger instead of the child who had grown inside of her for nine months. But in the second photo, Ana had softened slightly; she inclined her head toward her daughter with the barest, briefest flicker of a smile.

I wondered what had passed between them to weaken Ana's resolve. Did Stefany laugh or giggle? Did she flutter the lashes of her irresistible *ojitos*? Maybe Ana recognized her own face in Stefany's, or the face of Stefany's biological father. Or perhaps she had felt the invisible bond of blood.

Until that moment, I hadn't grasped the enormity of adoption: That for one woman to become a mother, another mother had to give up her child. That for every day that I lived with my daughter, another mother lived without her. And regardless of the birth mother's reasons—she was poor, she was alone, she had other children to care for—and no matter what we call it—surrender, relinquish, making an adoption plan—it still required one mother to give up her child to another.

Chapter 8

SEÑOR RODRÍGUEZ

June 2003. Three months after we got DNA, Yolanda organized a protest against the Hague adoption suspension. Her plan was for as many Americans as possible to march from their Camino Real hotel rooms to the Guatemalan Solicitor General's Office, the *Procuraduría General de la Nación*, or PGN.

PGN was where the Power of Attorney was registered at the beginning of a case. It was also step four in the adoption process—after DNA, pre-approval, and Guatemalan Family Court—the last major hurdle before the U.S. Embassy issued its pink slip. But it was a step that loomed ominously in the minds of adoptive parents and professionals because it was so unpredictable. Cases were assigned to a "reviewer" who approved or disapproved a case based on what seemed to be pure whimsy. Reviewers assigned *previos*, which meant the case was "kicked-out" until the *notario* provided the requested document: a new birth certificate or marriage license, a new medical report or letter attesting to the adoptive parents' character. Procuring such a document could take a week to several months.

Adoptive parents were regularly and repeatedly warned by their agencies *never* to go to PGN to check on a case. To do so was unthinkable, guaranteed to incur an agency's wrath.

Yet here was Yolanda, sending a group email with an open invitation. She visualized hundreds of parents walking down Boulevard de la Liberación, babies held aloft in our arms, chanting slogans and singing nursery rhymes. A news crew would record us marching behind our fearless leader, Yolanda, wielding a megaphone, the champion of children everywhere.

I signed up instantly.

But a week before the protest, Yolanda was forced to cancel. Except for Tim and me, no one else was willing to march.

"Everyone's scared," she wrote. "Scared they sabotage their case. Scared to fight for the children."

Tim and I weren't scared. Just sick of feeling helpless.

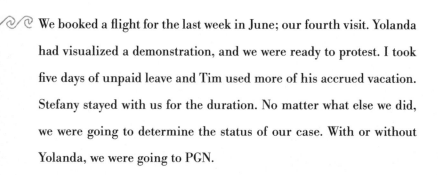 We booked a flight for the last week in June; our fourth visit. Yolanda had visualized a demonstration, and we were ready to protest. I took five days of unpaid leave and Tim used more of his accrued vacation. Stefany stayed with us for the duration. No matter what else we did, we were going to determine the status of our case. With or without Yolanda, we were going to PGN.

"*Hola*, Jessica and Tim," said Byron, the Camino Real shuttle bus driver who picked us up at the airport. "Here to get your baby?"

"Just visiting," Tim said.

"Here for the weekend?" said the front desk clerk. "Let's upgrade you to a suite."

An American mom comforted a crying Guatemalan baby on a sofa in the lobby. An American dad with a baby in a backpack walked by carrying two plastic bags of groceries. Because of the Hague, no new adoptions were being started, but from the looks of the Camino Real, plenty of parents continued to visit their children.

The waiter in the ninth-floor adoption lounge updated us on Nikki. She had lived in the hotel until February, when her *notario* finally completed the adoption and she left with her eighteen-month-old son. Ninth-floor housekeeping celebrated with a cake, and the spa comped her a manicure-pedicure.

When Lupe and Francisco dropped Stefany off at the Camino Real, I hardly recognized her. She was thirteen months old, becoming a toddler. Her cheeks had lost their chubby roundness. Her hair was in pigtails. The pink overalls that used to fit her like a clown suit barely covered her ankles. She was trimming down. The only thing that hadn't changed was her wary expression, the one that seemed to say, "*It's you two again. How long are you staying this time?*"

She pointed to Lupe when she heard the word *mamá*. She pointed to Francisco as *papi*. Even as I tried to convince myself that this attachment was good, I cringed at how Stefany hung on Lupe when she handed her over to me. My joy at having Stefany coexisted with her pain at leaving Lupe, and Lupe's pain at losing her.

PGN was straight up Boulevard de la Liberación, past the big Pollo Campero, Guatemala's wildly popular fast-food chain, and behind the Hotel Meliá; it was hard to find unless you knew where to look. The Camino Real concierge, Belbeth, drew us a map. We dressed up: Tim in a blue jacket and striped tie, and me in black wool trousers, a white blouse, and black ankle boots. Stefany looked adorable in a tiny pair of cargo pants appliquéd with a ladybug over each knee. I tucked a copy of our dossier in the backpack, plus diapers, formula, snacks, and water. Tim pushed the stroller.

In the pocketbook I wore strapped across my chest, I also carried a copy of the "foster mother paper." Lupe had given it to us with instructions to carry it always. Written in Spanish and stamped with an official PGN insignia, the foster mother paper named Lupe as Stefany's legal guardian. Our names weren't on it, but the fact that we possessed it established our relationship with Lupe.

Besides naming Ana, Lupe, and Stefany as parties, the paper listed the contact phone numbers for our *notario* and *mandatario*, the "senior" attorney on the case who must sign off on each document. Neither number worked.

Boulevard de la Liberación pulsed with the anarchy of Monday morning rush hour. Wildly painted, rehabilitated school buses, called "chicken buses," barreled down the street, each one spewing a ribbon of black exhaust. At every other corner, conductors swung out the front door to collect fares and call out stops while two boys hoisted themselves to the roof to toss down backpacks and luggage. Before the people on the bus could get off, clusters of commuters surged forward, elbowing one another aside to get on first.

"Are we nuts for doing this?" I called out to Tim as we stood stranded on an island in the middle of a traffic circle that possessed no discernible right of way. Drivers veered in what appeared to be efforts to hit us straight-on.

"You mean jeopardizing the life of our child?" He ducked to avoid getting smacked by a bus rearview mirror. "Definitely."

I tried to imagine Yolanda's hoped-for mob of American parents navigating the traffic as I jumped over a pothole. What was she thinking? The distance was walkable, but difficult. By the time we spotted PGN behind the Hotel Meliá parking lot, my blouse was stuck to my back and Tim's hair was plastered against his forehead. Stefany pressed her hands against her ears.

"We need to freshen up," I said. "We can't walk in there looking like this."

"This is no time for vanity." Tim turned me around and unzipped the backpack. "Here. Have a baby wipe."

Considering how largely PGN loomed in our consciousness, the building itself was surprisingly unimposing. Two stories high and sheathed with reflective windows, it could have been anywhere in any time, in any country. Only the words *Procuraduría General de la Nación,* written in brass letters on the ten-foot granite wall that surrounded it, confirmed its identity.

Tim and I had planned to walk in as if we belonged, and sure enough, the armed guard who paraded before the front wall touched the brim of his hat when we passed as though we were regular visitors. Behind the wall, a gardener was trimming roses in a raised flower bed that formed the letters "PGN." As I held the door open for Tim and Stefany, my heart pounded. In all my research on adoption, I had never read a word about how to facilitate your own case. I had no idea what to expect.

Six folding metal chairs were lined up against the left wall of the waiting room. A large sliding plastic window was on the right. White high-gloss paint had turned gray on the walls and the linoleum floor was scuffed.

A middle-aged female security guard with a gun holstered around her hips slouched on a chair by the door marked *ENTRADA*. Two attractive young women chatted on cell phones behind the reception desk. One hung up as we entered. Her eyes moved from Stefany's face to my face to Tim's face and back to the baby. I realized that for all the papers they processed in PGN, the staff might never have seen any adoptive families in the flesh. Maybe if they did, they would understand that we wanted only to become parents, just like anybody else.

I approached, armed with my Spanish dictionary. My command of the language was extremely basic, but I knew that any attempt to communicate was appreciated. Tim didn't speak any Spanish, so I was the designated mouthpiece. I did my best, if only to demonstrate I was willing to try.

My goal was to make sure our case predated the Hague deadline and thus fell under the old rules. I wrote our names—Tim's, mine, Yolanda's, Ana's, Stefany's—and showed them to the receptionist. I presented the foster mother paper, which named Lupe as Stefany's guardian. I pulled out our dossier, with its copy of our Power of Attorney, birth certificates, and marriage license. I said *gracias* and *por favor*.

The receptionist inspected the papers before pulling out a gray, clothbound book the size of a photo album. I saw that every single entry, including the column headings, was hand-written. I watched as she thumbed through the pages.

"We don't have a record of your case," she said.

The dirty linoleum tiles swam up at me. I leaned over the front of her desk, reaching for her ledger. "Check last July. That's when we signed the Power of Attorney."

Tim came up beside me. "What is it?"

"They don't have us registered."

"We have to be. They stamped our foster mother paper."

"I don't know." I felt hot and clammy. "I'm just telling you what she said."

"Oh, for Christ's sake." Tim grabbed the handles to the stroller and started wheeling Stefany around in circles.

The receptionist excused herself and slipped out the door marked ENTRADA. A minute later, she returned with Señor Rodríguez, Secretary General of PGN, a wiry, thin man with a thick fringe of brown bangs. His body seemed coiled with energy. He wore a braided gold bracelet on his wrist. His nose was a long, thin beak.

Rodríguez flipped through the clothbound book and picked up the copy of our dossier on the receptionist's desk. He picked up the foster mother paper, stamped by PGN, and glanced over it. As he looked down, his thick fringe of brown bangs flopped over his forehead hiding his face.

He said something to the receptionist, so fast I didn't understand a word. The security guard asked for our passports and patted us down. She directed Tim to take Stefany out of the stroller and patted her down, too. She waved us through the ENTRADA and directed us next door to Rodríguez's office.

The walls between Rodríguez's office and the ones on either side were see-through. Yards of gray canvas were draped from the ceiling in an effort to gain some privacy. The only wall uncovered was the one that faced outdoors. I did a double-take when I saw the roses in the "PGN" configuration and realized the building's reflective covering allowed Rodríguez to see us without our seeing him, as though we were specimens being observed through a two-way mirror.

Rodríguez gestured toward a swaybacked sofa that had seen better days and invited us to sit. As soon as we did, Stefany crawled from Tim's lap to mine, which I hoped Rodríguez noticed. No need for him to know that if Lupe were to show up, I would be forgotten. I was Stefany's first choice at the moment. And it was a small consolation.

Rodríguez's green metal desk was covered with scribbled-on yellow Post-it notes. A laptop computer, held together with gray duct tape, lay flopped open on one corner. His desk chair, mounted on wheels, was halfway across the room. As Rodríguez rolled it toward his desk I noticed that the seat bottom was reinforced with a thick square of cardboard.

Rodríguez fired a series of questions at us. He seemed incapable of speaking slowly, and I couldn't keep up. From somewhere in the building, a translator was summoned.

Lorenzo nodded hello, and cracked his neck. He placed his hands flat on Rodríguez's desk as if it were a pommel horse and hopped up to sit on a corner. As Rodríguez explained our situation, Lorenzo flexed his ankles, rotating each one in a figure eight.

"Where did you get this baby?" Lorenzo asked when Rodríguez was finished.

I instinctively put my hand on Stefany's head. I said, "The foster parents bring her to the hotel. Lupe and Francisco Garza. We're adopting her."

"Where did you get this paper?" Lorenzo rustled the foster mother paper.

"Same place," I said. "Lupe Garza."

The two men consulted. "We don't recognize the name of this *notario*," Lorenzo said. "Where did you find him?"

"Yolanda Sánchez," I said. No reaction from either of them. "From California?"

I felt Señor Rodríguez watching me closely. Maybe he realized that Tim and I were being taken advantage of. Maybe he was our ally.

I addressed Rodríguez directly in broken Spanish. "Yolanda is not good. Help, please."

"How much you pay?" he asked.

"A lot," I allowed. "A huge amount."

Rodríguez unpeeled a clean Post-it and passed it to me with a pen.

I looked at Tim, who nodded. Reaching my arms around Stefany's middle, I wrote the number "$25,000 U.S." and passed the note back to Rodríguez.

He shook his wrist before showing the note to Lorenzo, who also shook his wrist. Rodríguez opened his desk drawer and threw the Post-it inside.

At least everyone in the room knew we were paying full-fare.

Rodríguez turned toward Stefany. She was dropping Cheerios behind the back of the sofa cushions. "*Cuántos años tiene?*"

"*Un año.* Thirteen months."

"You first met baby today?"

"We met her when she was four months old."

"*Tienen otros niños?*"

I pulled Stefany onto my legs, bouncing my thighs slightly as I held each of her hands. "She's our one and only."

Rodríguez reached out a bony arm to chuck her under the chin. "*Es muy preciosa.*"

Precious was good.

Lorenzo stuck out his chest. "The laws are changing. PGN will not exist when we establish a new Central Authority."

I felt Rodríguez's eyes on my face, gauging my reaction. He seemed to be sizing me up based on what I said. Maybe he saw that I was sincere. It could be that he had seen too many Americans taken advantage of by their agencies, or we were the first ones to confront him directly. Maybe he thought we might pay him something. If he could get us some answers and end this ordeal, I didn't care.

"*Por favor, Señor.* We've been trying to adopt this baby for a year. They said our case isn't registered. The *notario's* phone is disconnected. We beg you to help us."

"But I don't know this man."

"What about Theodore?" I said.

"I know Theodore," Rodríguez said.

Tim pawed through the backpack for Theodore's contact information. Rodríguez set his telephone to speaker and punched

Theodore's number. I was shocked when I heard the tone of Theodore's voice as it filled the small office. Gone was his confident bluster. I had never heard him sound so accommodating.

Our *notario* was Simón Guerrero. Within a minute, Rodríguez had gotten his current number from Theodore and recorded it on a Post-it note. Within five minutes, Rodríguez had called Simón Guerrero and arranged for us to meet with him. He called Lupe and told her and Francisco to meet Tim and me at Pollo Campero, *pronto*. They needed to drive us downtown.

Tim and I were amazed at Rodríguez's success. He stood up and patted Stefany on the head. "*Suerte.*" "She's lucky."

"*Tenemos suerte.*" "We're the lucky ones."

At Pollo Campero we learned that Stefany loved spicy fried chicken with all the fixings. Black beans with bacon, mashed potatoes with gravy, french fries, coleslaw, rolls with butter. Stefany grabbed for everything, and slurped it down with deep gulps of grape juice. We gaped as she ate half of Lupe's flan and most of Vivian's ice cream—vanilla, smothered in a bright red topping that alleged to be strawberry.

The Garzas practically guffawed when I described how Tim and I ordered steamed rice and carrots for her at the Camino Real restaurant, and asked the kitchen if they had any organic beef they were willing to puree. Stefany licked sticky red sauce off each of her fingers and salt off the top of the salt shaker. She sucked on packages of sugar. Lupe ticked off a list of Stefany's other favorite foods—tortilla chips, pork tamales, spaghetti and meatballs, doughnuts. I was mildly appalled, but worse than that, I realized how little I knew about my own daughter. About as little as she knew about me.

Simón Guerrero's office was in the seedy part of Zone 1 in downtown Guatemala City, away from the new office towers and fancy cars, in the section where boys juggled on unicycles and begged for money as cars idled at stop lights. Because Francisco worked for the tourist bureau, *Inguat*, he knew the capital well, but apparently Guerrero's office was on a street Francisco was not familiar with. We spent half an hour cruising the boulevard, veering off to explore one false lead after another. Francisco thought nothing of backing up the wrong way down a one-way street if it got him closer to where he thought he should be going. Vivian navigated out the back window while I monitored the activity in the front seat, where Stefany sat seatbelt-less on Lupe's lap. A plastic Scooby-Doo figurine, a first birthday gift for Stefany, hung from the rearview mirror.

"Scooby-Doo, Scooby-Doo," Lupe said.

She tapped the figurine with her finger and encouraged Stefany to repeat the dog's name. When Stefany finally called out "Scooby," Lupe covered her face with kisses. I reached over the back seat and patted her on the head.

Tim said he was convinced that when we asked Guerrero the status of our case, the *notario* would claim to have submitted it to Family Court or PGN "two days ago" or "Tuesday." Tim had pegged Guerrero as a liar, and that was how liars behaved. With Vivian translating for her parents, Tim explained:

"When I first worked at the university, I was a doctor at a big hospital in San Francisco. Many of the patients used drugs." He pretended to inject a needle into a vein. "We call them 'drug addicts.' If I asked the drug addict, 'When's the last time you used?' the addict will always give the same answer. 'Two days ago,' or 'Tuesday.'"

Francisco gave a thumbs-up from the front seat; he and Lupe had had a similar experience.

"Guerrero's a drug addict?" I asked Tim.

"No, but he's a liar," Tim said. "'Two days ago' or 'Tuesday.' Then we'll know for sure."

Guerrero's office was in a former motel at the end of a dusty alleyway. There was no lobby, no directory, no buzzer—just a number on a door at the top of a narrow stairway. Francisco knocked while the rest of us waited in the alley. The door opened and a round-faced woman waved us in, "*Buenos días,*" she said. "*Me llamo Gilda.*"

We climbed the stairs and stepped into a hallway lit by a bare bulb dangling from a ratty cord. Our eyes adjusted to the darkness. The hallway smelled sharp, like body odor that had seeped into old clothes and would never launder out. The center of the floor drooped, worn down by a thousand passing feet. We pressed together. Nobody wanted to brush up accidentally against one of the grimy gray walls.

A door opened at the end of the hallway. Gilda gestured toward us, stepping aside to let us pass. Single-file, we tiptoed in.

A man young enough to be my son sat behind a metal desk in a three-piece blue suit, the gold cuff links of his white shirt flashing. He didn't look up or acknowledge us in any way. On the wall behind him were children's crayon drawings of sailboats and kites.

We settled into the office's only available seating, a tattered plaid sofa with a gray wool blanket stretched across the cushions. Gilda walked in and double-locked the door. First with a deadbolt, then with a brass chain. Tim squeezed my hand. We were locked in a room in Guatemala City and no one knew where to find us.

"How is it that the Secretary General of PGN called me in my office to arrange an appointment for you?" Guerrero said, revealing a mouthful of braces and perfect English.

He didn't introduce himself or ask us our names. He didn't comment on Stefany or the Garzas. He didn't try to hide the irritation in his voice. "This is not Argentina," he said. "This is not Paris. This is Guatemala. Things are different here."

He said we weren't to interfere with the adoption in any way whatsoever. To do so would jeopardize the outcome. We weren't to go to PGN. We weren't to communicate with the U.S. Embassy.

"Doctor," he said to Tim. "You are doctor, yes? Your case is now in Family Court. It will be in *Procuraduría* tomorrow, *mañana*. Or maybe next Tuesday."

I stared straight ahead, not daring to register Tim's expression, or the Garzas'. I just hoped Tim was smart enough to stay cool and collected. As a physician, he was trained to remain calm, but I didn't know if that applied to situations that involved threats to his own family. Silently, I begged him not to react.

The room was utterly quiet. No one seemed to be breathing.

"If we go to PGN on Wednesday," Tim asked, "the case will be there?"

Guerrero answered Tim as if he were a young child with limited capacity to comprehend. "There is no reason for you to go to PGN on Wednesday, or on Thursday or Friday. If you do, I can't predict what will happen."

The two men glared at each other. I telegraphed to Tim that if he angered Guerrero, I would never forgive him. This was not a game that we could win. The stakes were too high to risk trying. Tim looked away.

Guerrero pulled on his shirt sleeve and fiddled with a cuff link. "How about those Cleveland Browns? You think they'll get to the playoffs?"

"You follow the NFL?" Tim said haltingly. "How is it you're a Browns fan?"

"My wife's brother lives in Cleveland. We go every summer for two months."

"Aha," Tim said. "So that's why your English is so good."

Guerrero bowed slightly, accepting the compliment. He leaned back in his chair and crossed his hands over his vest. "Take my advice, Doctor. Don't interfere with our business. How do Americans say it? Don't go in over your head."

Chapter 9

THE U.S. EMBASSY

Wednesday morning, our fifth day in Guatemala, we asked Belbeth to call PGN to find out if Simón Guerrero had submitted the case. We hovered beside her concierge desk to listen to her half of the conversation, with me holding Stefany in my arms. I ignored the other adoptive parents who milled around the reception area, checking in and out.

Belbeth hung up the phone, shaking her head.

"But he promised," I said to Tim. I was angry at myself for trusting Guerrero in the first place. Stefany squeaked in alarm. I shushed her softly, thinking about how my anxiety must affect her.

Tim patted me on the back. "It's not that Guerrero's malicious. He says what we want to hear."

"You're defending Guerrero?"

"I'm being realistic."

We had heard from other Americans that Guatemalans considered it rude to tell someone an outright "no," which is why they so often responded with "*mañana*" and "*vamos a ver.*" "We'll see." Nevertheless, Tim's equanimity, which I appreciated in Guerrero's office, could also drive me mad. The fact that he was usually right just made me madder.

"Why don't you go to the U.S. Embassy?" Belbeth suggested. "They help Americans in trouble."

I advanced a step toward Tim, willing to reenlist him on my team.

"It's too late today," Belbeth said. "The line starts at six in the morning."

I circled Tim's neck with my free arm in a fake stranglehold. "Simón Guerrero said we shouldn't. What do you think?"

"I think we don't have a choice," Tim said.

The sidewalk was slick from a light drizzle as we joined the line of Guatemalan "runners" waiting outside the U.S. Embassy's side entrance at six the next morning. The runners were placeholders for attorneys and *notarios* who showed up later. Most were young men in their late teens or early twenties, with baseball caps pulled so low on their foreheads their eyes were invisible. The runner in front of us told us to get a number from the man at the security checkpoint. Tim trotted off, returning triumphantly a minute later with a wrinkled ticket.

"We're number six. Finished before lunch."

We high-fived each other, delighted to have figured out the system.

Around seven thirty, other adoptive parents began to trickle in, eager to receive their pink slip. A family received their pink slip after a case had been approved by PGN and the *notario* procured the baby's new Guatemalan birth certificate and passport. With pink slip in hand, parents took their baby to an Embassy-approved doctor for vaccinations and returned in the afternoon for an exit visa. Most families left the next day.

Many of the adoptive moms were with husbands and older children. Some were accompanied by their mothers and sisters and other extended family. Their babies and toddlers, parked under protective stroller hoods, nibbled on slices of bread and cubes of cheese from hotel breakfast buffets. Bundled in their cozy pink and blue jackets and soft slippers, the children already seemed part of their new families. I listened glumly as the adults chattered around us, swapping stories of what they considered "delays," a week or two here or there, a month at the most. I mentioned to one woman that it took us eight months to get DNA, but she wasn't listening. She was going home. What did she care?

A few feet away, on the other side of the sidewalk, a long line of Guatemalans waited for visas. They looked like the guests at the Camino Real: stylish clothes and expensive leather shoes. Although Guatemala was one of ten countries that represented more than fifty percent of all immigration to the United States, securing a visa was not easy. A Guatemalan citizen needed to prove he had a well-established residence; a logical reason for visiting the U.S. for a specific, limited time; and enough money to travel and pay for the trip him or herself. It was not surprising that less than ten percent of the 160,000 Guatemalans who entered the U.S. in 2000 did so legally.

As we passed through the security turnstile, I asked the runner in front of us what we were supposed to do when we got inside. We weren't there for a pink slip, but because we had a problem. He told me that there was only one immigration officer who handled troubled adoptions, Mandy Márquez, and sometimes she took an hour or more with a single case. The Embassy closed at four o'clock. Holding ticket number six was no guarantee we would meet with her.

"What happens then?" I asked.

"You come back tomorrow."

There were two waiting areas in the Embassy: one for Americans and one for Guatemalans. A uniformed guard herded us past an American flag and photo of the president into the American area. The room was plain: fifteen rows of folding chairs, with fifteen seats across. Lining the walls were seven bulletproof windows that looked like pawn shop tills, with an immigration officer standing behind each one. No vending machines, no water fountain, no magazines, no television. Nothing to detract from the room's intended purpose of waiting.

I turned to the runner. He pointed to a large wooden door at the end of the bulletproof windows. *"Márquez está adentro,"* he said. "Márquez is inside." A small brass numeral identified the door as #8.

The runner instructed us to wait in the first row with him and the other four Guatemalans waiting to consult with Márquez. The parents waiting for pink slips clustered in the seats near the bulletproof windows. I saw one couple in the back with a daughter who could not have been more than five months old. Despite having gotten up at the crack of dawn, the couple appeared well-rested and at ease; the baby was lively and burbling. An attractive Guatemalan woman in a form-fitting red suit and matching red eyeglasses accompanied them. The spiral binder on her lap told me she was an attorney or *notario*. The young age of the baby told me she was a good one.

I poked Tim in the ribs. "Imagine if we had her on our side, instead of Yolanda, who's ignored my emails all week."

"She does the work she's paid to do," said Tim.

"What would that be like?"

Tim slipped his arm around my shoulders and guided me to a seat in the first row. "We'll never know."

By noon, the pink slip crowd had rushed off to keep doctors' appointments. Mandy Márquez had twice peeked out from behind Door #8 to call ticket holders number one and two. She was dark-haired, pretty, friendly-seeming, but clearly harried—too young to be burned out but headed in that direction. Tim intercepted her, asking if it was worth our while to wait for her. "We're number six," he said. She directed him back to his seat with a promise that she was working as fast as she could.

"Ask one of the other officers," I urged.

Tim approached a window and the officer thrust a printed hand-out through the voice hole. The hand-out warned Americans not to ask questions about adoption at any window except Door #8.

"So glad our government is here to serve," Tim said.

We didn't dare leave the building for lunch, choosing instead to share a bag of corn nuts scrounged from a pocket in the backpack. Stefany drank formula and nibbled on Cheerios before falling into a fitful sleep on my lap. Tim and I each had toddled with her around the room's perimeter a few times and she was worn out. At one thirty, the pink slip crowd returned for their exit visas. The lawyer in the red suit and her family were back. When the couple received their baby's exit visa, they hugged the lawyer before hugging each other. They linked arms and exited the waiting room, the lawyer in the middle.

A woman dressed in a purple shift and purple bandanna tapped my shoulder and introduced herself as Norah. Her tiny daughter dozed in a portable carrier.

"Weren't you here this morning?" she asked. She was back to pick up her exit visa. She asked, "What's your daughter's name?"

"Stefany Mishell."

"I thought so. I remember her picture on Yolanda's website."

I felt so exposed, I literally recoiled. It was as though our personal family photo album had been opened for the world to see. Even Tim looked startled.

Norah reached under the edge of her bandanna to scratch her forehead. Her fingernails were bitten down to the quick. "I started with Yolanda about a year ago. A little girl named Caitlyn Mishell." She looked at Stefany. "Mishell is spelled a weird way, right? And Stefany, too."

Neither Tim nor I answered, but we didn't need to. Norah knew that what she had said was true.

"Didn't you notice that all the girls are named Caitlyn or Emily or Stefany? Those are names Yolanda thinks Americans like. There's another Stefany around here somewhere, I think." Norah scanned the room. "They must have left already."

The origin of Stefany's name had flummoxed Tim and me from the beginning, with both of us puzzled over why—or how—someone from Totonicapán would have chosen it. At the very least, *Estefanía* seemed a more likely choice. Neither one of us suspected it came from Yolanda.

Tim gestured toward Norah's sleeping baby. "Is this Caitlyn?"

"Janelle, actually."

"What happened to Caitlyn?"

"Supposedly, she went to a family in Connecticut. I gave up and got another agency. Lost fifteen grand, too." Norah hoisted the baby carrier onto her lap. "I'm a single mom. Dealing with Yolanda got too hard."

Tim and I stayed quiet. As adoptive parents, we knew intellectually that Stefany wasn't ours until the paperwork was finalized. But that didn't change how we felt about her. I brushed back Stefany's hair from her face and traced her ear with one finger. Stefany's beautiful, perfect ear, belonging only to her.

Norah inclined her head toward the back of the room. "I think that was our name." She stood up with the baby carrier suspended over her forearm. "I still think about Caitlyn." She chewed on the ragged skin around her thumbnail. "I hope she's okay."

Her shift swished against her legs as she walked to the window and set the carrier on the floor. The immigration officer slid the visa underneath the bulletproof window. I waved goodbye, but she left without turning back.

"We can change Stefany's name if you want," Tim said.

"Will it be too confusing?"

"She'll adjust."

I was torn because I liked the name Stefany, but I didn't know if I could ever say it without thinking of Yolanda, and whenever I thought of Yolanda, I felt angry and resentful. Ana's memory was of *Stefany*, regardless of whether she chose the name. If we changed the baby's name, would we take away what little Ana had to hold onto?

At three thirty, Mandy Márquez stuck her head out of Door #8 and announced number four before disappearing back inside. I was hysterical. The Embassy was closing in thirty minutes.

"We can't sit here for seven and a half hours and not be seen,"

I said to Tim. "What if we don't get in tomorrow? We're leaving on Sunday. We won't be back till Labor Day."

We'd run out of water and formula. Stefany was whiny, restless, and hungry. The runner in front of us had left, replaced by the middle-aged *notario* who paid him to stand in line. The smell of his acrid cologne was making me feel nauseated.

"We still have a half hour," Tim said. "Number four will probably be quick."

"Ask the guy in front of us if he'll change places. He just got here."

Tim hesitated.

"Ask him," I said again. I picked up Stefany and stood by Door #8 while Tim leaned over to the *notario*.

Márquez opened the door, smiling, with ticket holder number four behind her. "Number five," Márquez said.

I slipped out from behind Door #8 and cut in front of the *notario*, stepping inside the office with Stefany.

"But I am number five," the *notario* sputtered as he followed me in. Tim was close on his heels. Márquez came in last and closed the door to the now crowded office. The *notario* planted himself on the single stool. Tim and I stood in the corner with Stefany as Márquez walked around the metal desk and sat behind bulletproof glass. Because Márquez had never met Tim and me before, she probably assumed we were with the *notario*.

Tim spoke before the other man could. "You must have heard of

Yolanda Sánchez," he said. "Can't the Embassy stop her?" His voice was amplified by a hidden microphone secreted somewhere in the bulletproof glass.

Márquez's face remained neutral. "Not unless she commits a crime."

"Taking our money and not filing any paperwork. That's not a crime?"

"Yolanda may be unscrupulous, but she's not breaking any laws."

"Can't you switch us to another *notario*?" Tim pointed to the man on the stool. "Someone like this one here? We've got a facilitator headquartered in a hotel lobby and a *notario* practicing out of a fleabag motel."

Márquez tapped on her computer keyboard. "Give me your names again." She stared at the screen. "It says here that we issued our pre-approval three months ago on March 31. According to our records, someone named Gilda León picked it up a week later. What she did with it, I don't know."

We had Embassy pre-approval and DNA. The U.S. government was satisfied that Ana was Stefany's birth mother. Maybe Simón Guerrero hadn't been lying. Our case might really be in Family Court. We didn't understand why Yolanda hadn't shared with us this great news. Either she didn't know it herself, or it wasn't true.

Sunday night, we returned Stefany to the Garzas. Stefany had warmed up to us slightly, but even that had a downside. She wouldn't see us again for eight weeks, when we planned to visit over the long Labor Day weekend.

I wasn't sure visiting Stefany in the hotel for a weekend, or even a week, at a time was a good idea. It felt cruel to subject her to so much back-and-forth between us and the Garzas. While I couldn't pass up the chance to see her whenever possible, I worried about the effect of our sporadic visits. At almost fourteen months old, she was beginning to understand the concept of object permanence, if only because, in her life, there was none.

I was also concerned about Stefany's life when we weren't around. Seeing how easily she slurped down that sticky red sauce and licked salt straight from the shaker made me think she ate like that all the time. As an infant, her hair had been thick and black. It was thinner now, almost stringy. I didn't know, either, what her typical day was, or if she received any real exercise or mental stimulation. She had appeared so comfortable parked on the sofa in front of the TV at the Garzas' house, her head bobbing up and down to MTV. When I asked Lupe what Stefany liked to do, Lupe named her favorite cartoons: *Teletubbies, Plaza Sésamo, Los Cubitos.* Going to a playground or park never figured into the discussion.

Tim said, "You look like you're in a trance."

"I'm fine." I passed Stefany to Tim. "Except I forgot the new clothes."

After seeing the baby clothes in Yolanda's closet, I didn't trust that she would give the Garzas anything we sent her. Our habit ever since was to return Stefany with new clothes in larger sizes.

I reached into my pocket for my room key and made my way through the lobby to the elevators. On the way, I passed the now-familiar groups of adoptive parents meeting with their children for the first time. As I observed the affectionate tableaux, I questioned my own opinion about visiting. Could I imagine meeting Stefany for the first time during our pick-up trip? It was bad enough we missed her first teeth, her first words, and her first birthday. What if we had missed everything else, too?

In adoption, no solution seemed easy.

The elevator opened and I stepped inside. As I selected my floor, a wrist with a loose Rolex watch on it reached in to hold open the door.

"Theodore," I said, surprised. I hadn't seen him during our entire trip.

He waited until the door closed before speaking. His dark eyebrows were drawn across his forehead in a thick line.

"Who you think you are?" His voice was low, menacing. "You think you big-shot going to PGN office, yelling to get your baby out?"

His face was an inch away from mine, so close I felt a spray of saliva on my cheek. I backed into the corner, trying to make myself smaller.

"You think you smarter than Yolanda? PGN calls me up to ask questions. Who give you permission?"

I answered meekly: "Nobody."

The elevator shuddered to a stop on the ninth floor. The door slid open and the sound of clattering silverware and lively conversation drifted over from the adoption lounge. The smell of freshly brewed coffee filled the elevator. Theodore jammed his finger on the control panel.

The elevator lurched down. The floor numbers lit up as we descended.

"You think PGN gonna help you? They're not gonna help you. They laugh at you." He pulled a white handkerchief from his pocket and mopped his face.

"What are we supposed to do?" I asked. "Sit back and do nothing? Then what happens? They give Stefany back to her biological mother?"

Theodore stuffed the handkerchief into his pocket. "Her mother don't want her."

I pointed my finger under his nose. "How dare you talk about Stefany's biological mother that way."

I clamped my jaw shut to stop from adding *You fucker.*

"Maybe she grow up in orphanage," Theodore said. "Like Yolanda's daughter, Pilar."

The elevator doors opened onto a crowd of adoptive parents waiting to go up.

"Theodore!" one dad greeted him. Theodore thrust out his hand and clapped the dad on his shoulder. "Good to see you again." Smoothly he passed the dad and exited the elevator.

"Stefany will grow up in an orphanage over my dead body," I said loudly to Theodore's back. I felt the eyes of the other parents on me. "You hear that? Over. My. Dead. Body."

The doors shut and we ascended. I crossed my arms and stared at the floor to avoid engaging with the other parents. They were deeply quiet, in the way people are when they witness a car crash in the next lane on the freeway: intensely grateful they aren't involved. Every adoptive parent knew Theodore. They probably thought we got what we deserved by working with him in the first place. It was our fault for not practicing our due diligence.

The doors opened on the ninth floor and everyone piled out. I lagged behind the group before heading to our room, my thoughts racing: *How could Theodore have said such a thing? He never would have pulled something like that with Tim around. He had waited until I was alone because he knew I was easier to intimidate. There was no way I was letting my daughter grow up in an orphanage. I would kidnap her first.*

I picked up the bag of clothes for Stefany that I had left beside the bed. The room smelled like baby formula and baby soap. I wished I could bottle the scent and take it home with me.

Back in the lobby, I froze when I saw them together: Lupe clucking, Stefany jabbering in response. I gave Lupe the bag of clothes and kissed Stefany on the forehead. I chatted with Lupe about how the baby slept (not well), what she ate (nothing as delectable as Pollo

Campero), and what we did (paddled in the pool, toddled around the hotel room). Unspoken, but understood, was that with Lupe back in charge, order was restored. I wanted so much to be Stefany's mother.

I was the lone passenger in the Camino Real airport shuttle the next morning when Byron swung into the driver's seat. "Five more minutes," he announced, snapping open the daily newspaper.

I looked out the window for Tim. He was still at the reception desk, squaring the hotel bill.

I had passed Theodore on the way out, drinking coffee in the lobby with an adoptive family, charming them with his old-world manners, his tales of moving to Guatemala from Romania because in Romania they let the babies cry in their cribs. And, just like us, they believed everything he told them. Just like us, they had no choice.

I heard Byron asking me if our adoption was almost finished. I tried to answer him, but my voice caught in my throat. "Not even close," I said finally. "I feel like giving up."

Byron closed his newspaper and turned around in his seat to face me. Normally, he was a light-hearted young man, friendly and eager to laugh. I had never seen him so serious.

"Can I tell you a story?" he asked. "Because you seem like a nice person, maybe you can hear it."

I shrugged noncommittally, not wanting to appear impolite.

"We had a three-year-old son. Our first boy, Ricardito. He was on a bus with my wife, sitting on her lap. On their way to his grandma's, around last Christmas. At one of the stops, a man got on and asked for everyone's wallet. People were taking too long, so to make them hurry, he pulled a gun. A bullet went off." He pointed to his left shoulder. "Shot my son through the lung here."

I was so shocked, it took me a moment to react. "He was killed?"

"He bled to death with my wife holding him." He turned back around in his seat, talking not to me, but to the windshield in front of him. "At night I wake up and hear my wife beside me, crying. I can't help her. Nothing I do can make her stop remembering."

"Did they find the guy who did it?"

Byron picked up the newspaper and rattled it over the back of his seat. "Look at the headlines," he said, forcing me to see the front page. "Killings, murders, drive-by shootings. Every day in Guatemala so many people die. Nobody gets caught."

He folded the paper onto the dashboard. "So please. Don't ever say you will give up on your child. Especially to me."

He wiped his eyes and turned on the ignition key.

Tim bounded through the lobby door, glancing at the hotel bill a final time before creasing it down the middle. Byron revved the engine as Tim climbed aboard.

"What's going on?" Tim looked from me to Byron. "What happened?"

I shook my head as Tim sat beside me and Byron pulled out from the curb.

As we wended toward the airport, I knew that if I was going to be Stefany's mother, I needed to be her mother. And if being her mother meant I had to move to Guatemala to finish her adoption, that was what I would do. Nikki had done it. I had heard other mothers talk about it, too.

If Yolanda and Theodore wouldn't finish the adoption, we would finish it ourselves.

Tim didn't miss a beat when, on the plane ride home, I informed him of my decision. If something happened to Stefany while I was away from her, I would never forgive myself. My parents and our families also understood. The consensus was that we had given Yolanda and Theodore adequate opportunity to succeed. It was time to take matters into our own hands. For a few anxious seconds after everyone agreed, I reflected on how little Spanish I spoke and how far away from emergency medical care I would be. At the Camino Real, Tim had always taken the lead, running the bath water and sterilizing the baby bottles. What if she got a cold or a fever? I would be in charge.

But those fears were fleeting. Stefany would live with me. I would finally be her mother.

The logistics were easy. My boss accepted my resignation with regret and my coworkers organized a baby shower/going-away party that reminded me how fond I was of my job and my colleagues. But as I unpinned the adoption flow chart and photo montage of Stefany above my computer, I knew I'd made the right decision. Yes, we had DNA and Embassy pre-approval, but that had taken a year. I needed to be closer to the action.

I contacted a real estate agent, Nadine, who was recommended to me by other mothers at the Camino Real. She found me an apartment in Antigua, forty-five minutes north of Guatemala City, where Stefany had been born. The apartment came equipped with its own washing machine, microwave oven, and Paola, a housekeeper who cleaned five half-days a week. The cost was $1,100 per month plus utilities. I asked Nadine how long a lease I should sign—one month or two?—but she recommended I leave the lease open-ended. "From my observation," she said, "you could be here for a while."

Tim and I spent our last night together in bed. Our love-making had always been passionate and athletic, but now it was infused with the urgency that arose with impending separation. We were desperate to be close to each other for as long as we could. Being with Tim gave me strength, and it was as though I wanted to fill myself with as much of his essence as I could.

I trusted Tim, but because we'd both failed at previous marriages, I took nothing for granted.

Chapter 10

GOODBYE TO LUPE GARZA

Late July 2003

Lupe was already crying when she entered the Camino Real lobby carrying Stefany. The doorman bowed as she passed, and the cluster of adoptive parents, waiting for the shuttle to the airport, parted. Vivian walked beside her mother, one arm around Lupe's broad shoulder, plucking tissue after tissue from a small purse-size packet. Francisco kept a respectful distance behind, his hands clasped in prayer.

Nobody knew what to say. I kissed Vivian on the cheek and hugged Francisco before reaching for Lupe. But she and Stefany were an immoveable mass, too wide and unyielding for me to get my arms around. I settled for stooping to kiss Stefany's forehead and blinking my good wishes to Lupe. Lupe clutched Stefany as though they'd fallen into a swift river and were being swept downstream.

Nadine was due to pick me up in an hour, at noon. I had planned to spend the hour drinking a final cappuccino in the hotel restaurant with Stefany. I didn't want to see what Lupe felt, her hurt and her loss, the sudden cool emptiness in her arms where Stefany's warm body had been. I didn't want to think about Lupe's half-empty bed, the spot on the pillow she told me she reserved for Stefany, assigning Francisco to the couch. The Garzas had never fostered a child for so long, long enough that the house was filled with memories of her: a strand of her black hair across the pillow, the yellow duck waiting on the edge of the bathtub, the candle from her first birthday cake. I knew that pain of absence.

The Camino Real had an unwritten rule that foster parents were not to go beyond the lobby to the guest rooms, adoption lounge, or swimming pool. But I wasn't coming back to the Camino Real any time soon. I glanced around at the lobby's polished marble floor, the uniformed bellmen, the American families on the mauve silk sofas. We had met at this exact place almost a year ago, and I had felt so exposed. There was no way I could say goodbye here, with so many people coming and going.

"Let's sit outside," I suggested.

Vivian and I guided Lupe through the lobby and out through the side door to one of the round teak tables under an umbrella. We held her under both elbows as she swooned into her seat, still gripping Stefany to her chest. Vivian and I sat on either side of her. Francisco stood at the edge of the pool, staring into the smooth surface.

"Please tell Lupe she can visit in Antigua." I handed Vivian a card with our address.

I also gave Vivian a small photo album filled with pictures from our visits. Vivian bit her lip as she opened the album on the table in front of Lupe's chair. There we were, smiling in the hotel lobby, at the Garzas' house, in the nearby Pollo Campero. "*Mi hermanita*," Vivian said as she paused at a photo of her holding Stefany by her fingers as Stefany took a few uncertain steps. "My little sister." Lupe glanced down at the picture briefly before turning away.

Stefany was anxious and watchful. She had been handed over between us for a year, yet she somehow seemed aware that this good-bye was different. With a slow, repetitive motion she raised her wrist to her lips to suck on her sleeve, reassuring herself she was present and alive, familiar. Her eyes were rimmed with circles of exhaustion. She kept them open as if afraid of who might disappear if she closed them.

Francisco walked over to the table, his mouth twisted into an expression of discomfort. When I had first met Francisco, he reminded me of a samba dancer, lithe and narrow-hipped, light on his feet. Today he seemed heavy and slow.

"*Con permiso, señora.*" I knew he was nervous because he never called me *señora*. From the beginning, we were Jessica and Tim. Francisco jingled the change in his pockets. "Theodore not pay Lupe for six month," he said.

I looked to Vivian for confirmation.

Vivian reached down to her pocketbook and produced a plastic bag filled with receipts. "Not for the doctor, either."

I borrowed a pen from Vivian to make some calculations. "That's $950." I wondered whether Francisco was telling the truth. I trusted him more than I trusted Yolanda or Theodore, but that didn't mean much. Francisco was disappointed when he asked for a car and we said we couldn't buy one. I began to explain that Lupe should have been paid from our adoption fees, before realizing that it didn't matter where the money should have come from. What mattered was that Lupe hadn't been paid.

I opened my hands to show they were empty. "I need to go to the bank. I don't have that much cash."

A waiter hurried out to us, a tea towel folded over his arm, but nobody was hungry. The Garzas ordered Cokes for themselves and lemonade for Stefany. I ordered a cappuccino. When the drinks arrived, Lupe lifted Stefany up to the table so she could sip her lemonade through a straw. They watched closely while she drank.

"*Mira.*" Francisco's face broke into a grin as Stefany slurped the last sip of lemonade, looking for more. He shook his finger. "*No más.*"

Stefany gripped the glass from Lupe and turned it upside down. The straw bounced off the table and onto the ground, while the last drops of lemonade spilled onto Lupe's lap. Vivian opened her eyes wide. "Uh-oh," she said to Stefany. She pretended to slap her cheeks with her open palms, exaggerating her dismay. Stefany chuckled.

I forced myself to chuckle, too. Stefany so rarely laughed when she was with Tim and me that I wanted to encourage her. Once she had laughed in the swimming pool as a big boy jumped in the shallow end, his legs drawn up tight in a cannonball, right beside where we stood. Water had splashed onto her eyes and face, surprising her. It pained me to realize how few times I'd heard the sound of my daughter laughing.

Vivian bent to scoop up the straw and present it to Stefany. Stefany put the straw in her mouth and blew through it, aiming directly for Lupe's neck. Lupe lifted her shoulder to brush away the tickle. Stefany blew through the straw again. Lupe pulled Stefany closer.

"I should get the money," I said, relieved for the excuse to leave.

Twenty minutes later, I was back at the swimming pool. Francisco stood beside us with his arms crossed, scanning the area for anyone who might be watching. I quickly passed an envelope stuffed with cash to Vivian. She squeezed the envelope as though she could determine its value by its heft, and thrust it into her purse.

Lupe's body was rounded protectively over Stefany's, but as we executed our transaction, she lifted her head enough that she saw what was going on. As soon as the money was tucked in Vivian's purse, Lupe pressed her cheek against Stefany's and rocked side to side. She knew it was time to go.

I had made a decision not to feel anything because I wasn't going to make it through the day otherwise. This was a business for

Lupe, I told myself. She fostered children to make money. I helped Lupe out of her chair and led her through the lobby and out to the curb. Francisco and Vivian followed. The doorman hailed a cab as I thanked each of the Garzas.

Stefany's face was wet with Lupe's tears when Lupe finally handed her to me. "*Mi niña, mi amor, mi hija,*" Lupe said. "My little one, my love, my daughter."

She climbed into the back seat of the taxi beside Vivian and Francisco and the driver closed the door. I stood, waving, on the curb with Stefany. "Bye-bye, Lupe."

"Mommy's here," I murmured into Stefany's ear. She felt light and stiff in my arms, like a figure carved from balsa wood.

I was so afraid of Yolanda's reaction to my moving that I didn't tell her of my plans until after the Garzas had left. I sat in a secluded corner of the lobby so nobody could hear my conversation and read from a script I'd written. For courage, I held onto Stefany.

I needn't have worried. Yolanda wasn't the least bit concerned that I was taking Stefany away from the Garzas to live with me in Antigua. "Hold onto the foster mother paper," she said. "You'll need it if the police ask questions." The official policy by Guatemalan authorities regarding Americans who fostered was "don't ask, don't tell." Yolanda advised me to keep a low profile.

What concerned Yolanda most was money. Four months into the

Hague suspension, with few families starting adoptions, Yolanda had no income. She had been forced to sell her home in Los Angeles and move into a smaller one in North Hollywood. She didn't care that I reimbursed the Garzas from my own pocket, either.

"They take advantage of you," she said bitterly. "Theodore pay them, I'm sure."

I didn't know where the truth lay, and at that point, it was irrelevant. $950 was a small price to pay for the care the Garzas had given Stefany.

"Of course, you pay everything now because you live there," Yolanda added.

"Of course," I agreed, thinking *haven't we all along?*

"I admire you, Jessica," Yolanda said. "You move to Guatemala to get your baby out. Maybe I should do the same, for Pilar."

For a moment I felt more sympathetic toward her. Like me, she went to sleep every night knowing her daughter was growing up far away without her. But my sympathy was short-lived. Yolanda had brought unnecessary chaos to my child's life and the lives of untold numbers of other children. She had no business facilitating adoptions. Somebody should have stopped her long ago.

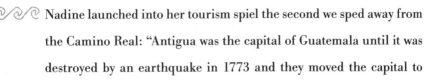 Nadine launched into her tourism spiel the second we sped away from the Camino Real: "Antigua was the capital of Guatemala until it was destroyed by an earthquake in 1773 and they moved the capital to

Guatemala City. In 1944, the government declared Antigua a national monument." Forty miles later, as we neared Antigua, her enthusiasm was undiminished. For Nadine, who had grown up in the frozen tundra of Edmonton, Canada, living in Guatemala was paradise.

With her straight posture and stylish, strawberry blonde wedge haircut, Nadine exuded energy. I asked polite questions and made appropriate comments. Within minutes, she confided that she was forty-eight years old and married to a Guatemalan businessman ten years younger than she. They had chosen not to have children. Nadine experienced motherhood vicariously, by finding Antigua apartments for adoptive "mums." Eight such moms were currently living in Antigua. One of them, Kendra, was also from the Bay Area. She was a single mom who moved down a month ago and telecommuted as a soil specialist for an environmental company. Her daughter had been left at an orphanage.

Stefany was safely strapped in a car seat. My cell phone was charged. Our luggage was stowed in the trunk, along with a few bags of groceries I had picked up at *Hiper Paiz*, the mega-store outside Guatemala City. While Nadine waited in the car with the baby, I had run in to buy my usual items—cereal and coffee, eggs, pasta, cheese, and tomato sauce.

Twenty-four hours earlier, I had kissed Tim goodbye at the San Francisco Airport. He promised to call me at seven every morning to check in. I had assured him I'd be fine. With any luck, we would be a family in the legal sense within six weeks. I was the one who had to make that happen. Tim was depending on me.

Looming on the horizon was a billboard of a sixty-ish light-skinned man with wavy hair and a neatly trimmed mustache. He was dressed in a blue denim shirt of the working class and wearing a comforting expression. The caption across the bottom of the billboard read "*Con Berger ganamos todos.*" "With Berger, we all win."

"My husband's last name is Berger, too," I said.

"We pronounce it *Ber-jér*. Emphasis on the last syllable. He's running for president."

"He's whiter than I am."

"Oh yes," Nadine said. "They all are."

She told me that Berger's chief opponent was General Efraín Ríos Montt, the country's former dictator who had come into power in the 1980s with a "scorched earth policy" against the indigenous. More than four hundred villages were obliterated during his tenure. In this election, he was giving away free stoves and bicycles to the same communities in exchange for their votes. The voters were the children of the population he tried to wipe out. No one seemed surprised by this. People did what they had to do.

We'd driven uphill for almost thirty minutes, through the capital city and its surrounding suburban sprawl, littered ankle-deep with trash and cluttered with strip malls. Over the crest the scenery changed. We descended into a lush green valley. The dense foliage felt undisturbed and primordial. The clear outline of the trees could have been drawn with the sharp point of a calligrapher's pen.

Nadine opened the driver's side window and breathed the pine-scented air. "This is what made me fall in love with Guatemala."

I reached over the back of my seat to squeeze Stefany's toes, and her foot twitched. Her suspicious expression hadn't changed. How long before she wasn't disappointed that I was not Lupe?

Nadine said, "I see that with the other mums. It's very tough in the beginning."

Nadine probably saw more adoptive mothers and children at this exact moment in their relationship than most adoption professionals. If she said it was tough for everyone, undoubtedly it was. The distance I felt between Stefany and me was normal, something we could work through over time. Nadine's words reassured me.

We drove a few miles in silence as Nadine navigated the narrow, twisting road. We passed a thin, stooped man hauling a bundle of sticks on his back. A cow grazed on the side of the road, tethered to a stake. At an outdoor washing pool, three women leaned over the water's edge scrubbing clothes.

"Maybe you know. Do a lot of people change their baby's names?" I asked.

"Depends on the family. It's a personal choice." She shifted gears. "What names are you considering?"

"Caroline. Francesca. Olivia." I paused between each name so

Nadine could consider it. "Olivia works across every culture," she said. "That's my vote."

Nadine turned off the paved road at a sign announcing *"La Antigua."* The car bumped onto a cobblestone street the color of goldenrod. In the distance were Antigua's three volcanoes: Agua, Fuego, and Acatenango.

The stucco buildings along Antigua's narrow street were painted with faded washes of oranges, blues, pinks, and yellows that probably once glowed like neon. We passed so closely I saw the pineapple patterns on their carved front doors. A steady procession of pedestrians promenaded along the raised sidewalks, dipping their heads to avoid the fancy wrought-iron filigree that protected the shuttered windows. Each corner revealed the tumbled-down ruins of a church, or a view of a volcano, or the sight of an indigenous mother with her baby in a hand-woven sling.

Antigua proper was a mile or so in diameter, laid out in a grid pattern. The *avenidas* ran north-south and the *calles* east-west, information that might have been helpful if any of the streets had had signs on them.

"This is *Parque Central*," Nadine said as we approached a large outdoor plaza planted with leafy trees. "Americans call it 'the Square.'"

A horse and buggy clopped along the edge of the park, while a man pushed a cart decorated with hand-painted pictures of ice cream cones. Small fountains stood on each of the park's four corners. A large fountain decorated with bare-breasted mermaids, *Las Sirenas*, dominated the middle. We drove by a yellow church and turned down a side street.

"Here we are on Fourth Avenida Sur. If you get lost, look for the biggest volcano, Agua."

A towering, snow-capped mountain shimmered in the distance. "Not active, I hope," I said.

Nadine stopped in front of a small attached house as auburn as an autumn leaf. "I'll give you Kendra's cellular number. You'll like her. She's a few blocks away."

"I'll call her first thing tomorrow," I said.

I hopped out of the car and regarded the house, which Nadine called a *casita*. Red geraniums spilled from baskets hanging in the front windows. Wooden shutters on three windows were opened behind the black wrought-iron grilles. A brass doorknob in the shape of a crouching lion graced the front door. I took Stefany out of the car and held her up to see it.

The *casita* was much bigger than it appeared from the outside.

The entrance hallway opened onto a generous living room with a cathedral ceiling and stone fireplace. Patterned wool rugs lay scattered over the red tile floor.

The dining room was large enough to hold a table that seated eight and a second fireplace. Paintings by Guatemalan artists were hung on every wall. The kitchen was small but functional, and included a wood-burning oven. Nadine pulled aside a curtain under the sink to show me the chef's knives and fancy silverware.

Sliding glass doors opened onto a courtyard that featured a traditional *pila*, or outdoor concrete sink, used for laundering clothes and linens. Most older homes featured *pilas*, Nadine explained, even when they had indoor plumbing. Many Guatemalans preferred to launder their clothes by hand.

The *casita's* spiral staircase to the master suite was waxed, solid mahogany, and much more slippery than I was used to. Carefully holding Stefany in one arm, I pressed my other hand against the stairwell to steady myself as we ascended. Across from the queen-sized bed, another sliding glass opened onto a charming patio, ideal for relaxing with a glass of wine. Beyond the patio was an unobstructed view of Volcano Agua, its base as wide as Antigua.

"I wouldn't mind living here forever," I said. "Not sure how my husband would feel about that, though."

"I could live here myself," Nadine agreed. She fluffed her strawberry blonde hair with her fingers. "I don't mean to rush off, but I'm sure you'd like to unpack and put away your groceries."

I walked Nadine down to the front door. "I couldn't have done this without you," I told her. She waved away my thanks. "Call Kendra," she said.

The lock on the front door clicked shut. Stefany jerked to attention.

"Here we are," I said.

My daughter was no longer an abstraction—a little girl meant for Tim and me, somewhere in the world—but a living, breathing child. The tenderness I felt toward her almost knocked me down. As I pulled her close, she twisted her body back and forth and slid down my legs toward the floor. Not the response I was hoping for, but I understood. The day must have been the most confounding one of her short life.

"You probably want to move around, huh." I picked up the grocery bags. "What do you think of the name 'Olivia'? I'm going to try calling you that."

She was staring at the floor.

I crouched to see what was so fascinating.

A battalion of red ants was advancing from underneath the front door. I had read an article about a type of red, tropical ant that swarmed a human body and ate it alive. Olivia stuck out her finger. The ants instantly marched up.

I grabbed Olivia under her arms. Her body felt heavy and leaden. Her diaper was drenched and sodden, completely absorbed with pee. It dropped down to her ankles and onto the floor, taking her pants down with it. In the excitement of the day, I had forgotten to change her diaper.

I swatted at her finger to brush off the ants. Ants landed on the floor, running in circles.

I rushed with Olivia, bare-bottomed, to the kitchen, and filled a pot with water. Water sloshing, I ran back down the hallway, opened the door and kicked the diaper onto the sidewalk. Ants floated in a puddle in the middle of the hallway. Ants scurried toward the front door. I squished the few remaining stragglers under my shoes and ground them into the floor.

I had taken custody of my daughter, only to subject her to an ant attack within the first hour. "I'm a better mother than this," I told her. "This is not a good indication."

Olivia jammed her fist into her mouth. Her eyes were wide open.

My skin felt prickly and creepy, as if ants were crawling over it, but I could not allow myself to become sidetracked. Olivia needed a diaper.

I took Olivia upstairs, spread out the changing pad, and laid her on the bed.

Lifting her bottom, I slid a diaper underneath and began to fasten the tabs.

Olivia grunted sharply. "*Ehh.*" She glared up at me, reaching down to pull off the diaper.

"What is it, honey? *Qué pasó?*"

I fastened the diaper tab; she unfastened it. I fastened it again; she unfastened it again. Then I remembered that Lupe had always put diaper rash cream on first. Tim did, too.

She was much more agreeable after I slathered on the cream. I couldn't believe how incompetent I was.

"*Hola*, Olivia." I scrunched up my nose.

She wasn't buying it.

"*Hola*, Olivia Stefany. Stefany Olivia?"

The name change would not happen overnight. I dressed Olivia in dry clothes and carried her to the kitchen where I berated myself for not buying tortillas at *Hiper Paiz*. Nadine had said the best tortillas were sold on the street in Antigua, but what street? Any tortillas would have been better than none.

Olivia sat on my lap and ate elbow noodles with her fingers. I speared mine with a fork. In between bites, I smoothed her hair back from her face. We had never known for sure whether the Garzas were feeding her the formula we gave them. Other mothers at the Camino Real told me foster mothers often sold the formula or saved it for a family member. Too late to do anything about that.

What was clear was that Olivia needed protein. I hacked off a chunk of parmesan cheese and placed it on her tongue. She closed her mouth around it, licking her lips. I cut off another chunk and popped it in. I didn't realize she wasn't swallowing until she began to choke.

I pounded on her back between her shoulder blades. A thick wad of cheese indented faintly with teeth marks landed in my hand. I pushed the cheese to the other side of the table and concentrated on the noodles. One night without protein wasn't going to kill her. One night with it almost did.

I glanced at the clock on my cell phone. Two hours until bedtime.

It was too dark to explore the neighborhood and if I let Olivia crawl on the floor, who knew what trouble she might find? I counted twelve electrical outlets—uncovered—that were exactly the right height for Olivia to stick her fingers into. The waxed stairs were an invitation for her to fall backward and crack open her head. If she accidentally bumped into a sliding glass door, a million splintered shards could take out her eyes. No wonder Lupe depended so much on TV.

We could have played children's games if I had known any. She didn't understand a word I was saying.

"Bath time," I announced. "Upstairs."

I pointed to the ceiling. "*Arriba.*" And to the floor. "*Abajo.*"

Olivia seemed puzzled by my pronunciation.

I almost wept with relief when I discovered a white, child-sized plastic bathtub on our bathroom counter upstairs, although I had never given Olivia a bath without Tim beside me. I wished I'd paid more attention. The cardinal rule, I knew, was to never turn your back. With my eyes on Olivia, I placed the small tub inside the bath tub and filled it with water. I undressed her on the tile floor and stood her carefully inside. She drew into herself, hugging her arms around her torso and squeezing her legs together. I picked up a few drops of water and flicked them gently onto her arm.

She stared into my eyes. She looked so small and vulnerable. Finally, she lowered herself into the water, bending first one knee and then the other, the water barely covering her tiny thighs and bottom. She gripped the edges of the plastic tub.

"*Pa. Pa,*" she said.

"*Papi?* You want *papi?*"

That wasn't it. It was the small rubber duck we had given her, which, like everything else, stayed behind with Lupe. *Patito.*

I had brought another yellow rubber duck from San Francisco—not exactly like the original, but the only one I could find. Where the old duck had a hole in the bottom, the new duck was solid. While the old duck had let out a satisfying squeak when squeezed, the new duck was silent.

I held up the new duck at Olivia's eye level. "Ducky. *Patito.*"

I set the duck in the tub and tapped him from behind his tail. He floated toward Olivia's leg. "Ducky swimming."

Olivia ignored the duck. I tapped him again. This time, the duck bumped up against Olivia's leg and bobbed backward on the swell before bumping her again.

"*Qué lindo,*" I said. "Cute ducky."

Olivia's right hand emerged from under the water and reached for the duck, which fit neatly into her palm. She squeezed him once. Nothing. She squeezed again. No squeak. She shook the duck beside her ear, grabbed it in both her hands and squeezed and squeezed. She threw the duck into the water with an expression that said, "What else have you got?"

Two hundred diapers and five jumbo cans of iron-fortified formula, and one crummy bath toy that didn't even squeak. I wiggled her big toe and spoke the only nursery rhyme I knew all the words to, "This little piggy went to the market. This little piggy stayed home."

Olivia leaned forward and looked at her feet.

"And this little piggy." I opened my eyes wide. "Went wee, wee, wee all the way home." I ran my fingers up her leg to her chin. No reaction.

We were awake until almost midnight. I read *Goodnight Moon* and *Moo, Baa, La La La* until my throat was hoarse. I tried to rock her to sleep. Olivia writhed and squirmed. She snuffled and whimpered. She crawled across the bed.

I scooped her up and padded through the dark bedroom, downstairs through the dining room and into the kitchen.

"Are you hungry?" I asked and measured formula into a bottle and poured in the water. Holding Olivia in my left arm, I attempted to force in the nipple. Olivia clamped her mouth shut and pushed away the bottle.

Then she started screaming. And I had no idea how to make her stop. I set the bottle in the sink and staggered with her back upstairs.

How long I had dreamed of this day, the first together as mother and daughter. But this was a nightmare. Olivia bit my cheeks and pulled my hair. She kicked and clawed. Whatever I was offering, she didn't want. She was inconsolable.

I needed to get hold of myself. I had to breathe my way through this experience until it became a part of our past, one element in our shared story. Lurching into the bedroom, I stretched out on the bed and wedged Olivia between my body and the wall. She could fight me all she wanted. I wasn't letting her go.

PART TWO

Chapter 11

KENDRA

Sometime in the middle of the night, firecrackers exploded and packs of dogs started barking from what seemed like every direction. Olivia slept through the cacophony, and I pulled a pillow over my ears to drown out the din. If there was a noise ordinance in Antigua, it didn't seem very effective.

I woke up with Olivia beside me, still asleep. I propped myself up on one elbow to see out the sliding glass door. The volcano was huge and seemed to be smoking. Wispy clouds streaked the sky. A bell in a clock tower tolled six times. A bus rolled over the cobblestones. The conductor called out *"Guate, Guate,"* en route to the capital. Everything felt different.

Olivia stirred in bed beside me, her brown cheeks flushed with sleep. She was such a beautiful girl. Tim and I agreed that of all the babies we'd seen at the Camino Real hotel, she was the most striking. We couldn't believe how lucky we were.

"Hola, niña," I said.

She looked at me with curiosity, which was an improvement. *What's this new place?* she seemed to be asking. *Where are we now?* I didn't see fear in her face, which felt like a breakthrough. I directed her attention to the volcano outside and sang my version of the "Good morning" song from *Singin' in the Rain*. She rewarded me with a small smile. I told her I'd sing to her tomorrow, and every day after that.

Olivia must have been starving. Yesterday she had eaten almost nothing. After I changed her diaper, I bundled her in my arms and padded cautiously downstairs. We ate breakfast with her on my lap. I spoke slowly, describing my every action. "Mommy's feeding Olivia an egg. Mommy's pouring her cereal into a bowl. Mommy's drinking coffee. Mommy's drinking more coffee."

Olivia was so quiet I peered into her face to make sure she hadn't dozed off. Just the opposite. She was watching my every move, hanging onto my every word, as if she were trying to make sense of this new reality. I kept talking.

At 7:00 AM, Tim called. "How are my girls?"

"What do you think of the name 'Olivia'?" I asked.

"Love it," he said.

After I described the previous night's events, he assured me that the last twenty-four hours were the worst Olivia and I would ever spend together. Today would be better. He encouraged me to call some of the other mothers so they could show me around Antigua. No need to go it alone.

My parents called next on speaker. "What's the weather like?" asked my father.

"So far, so good."

"How's the baby?" asked my mother.

"Terrific. She's growing. You should see her legs. Long and lean."

"Maybe she'll be a Rockette like her grandmother," my father said. "Wouldn't that be something? The first Guatemalan Rockette."

"How tall is she?" asked Mom.

"I don't mean now," my father said. "When she gets older."

My mother interrupted. "When are you coming home?"

"I just got here."

"Hold the phone up to the baby," said Dad. They called out, in unison, "We love you!"

"We love you, too," I said.

Kendra answered her phone on the first ring.

"I hope I'm not calling too early," I said.

"Oh, pshaw," said Kendra. "What's sleep? I've got a five-month old. How about we meet at Conexión to check email. Right next door to the Fuente Café. Say in an hour?"

"See you then."

I looked at my Antigua map and plotted our route. Before meeting Kendra, we could explore Antigua.

Nadine had recommended I bring a baby jogger because a

conventional stroller wouldn't roll over Antigua's cobblestone streets, so I had schlepped one from San Francisco. Twice I had had to explain why I was checking a baby jogger when I had no baby, but I was glad to have it. I thought of it as my car, able to transport everything I couldn't stuff into a backpack. I strapped Olivia into the low-slung seat. She looked like a driver in a Formula One race car.

The morning was almost chilly, the sky more drab than blue. Guatemala's slogan, "Land of Eternal Spring," was misleading, I discovered, especially at the elevation in Antigua. "Eternal Fall" felt more like it, at least at that hour. I draped a blanket over Olivia's legs, turned right, and headed toward the Square. The streets were empty; the shutters on the surrounding houses were closed tight. The only sounds I heard were the wheels of the jogger.

With each step, I felt more in control, more like living in Guatemala would be an adventure. I'd educate myself about its painting and weaving and learn more about its history. When Tim arrived, we would visit the places featured in my guidebook: Lake Atitlán, Chichicastenango, and Tikal. As Olivia got older, she would know how enthusiastically I had embraced her country of birth.

On the east side of the Square was the Cathedral, accessible by stone steps that ran the length of its block-long facade. I loved that it was called simply "the Cathedral," without any other descriptive name or embellishment. Antigua had many churches—*La Merced, Las*

Capuchinas, Hermano Pedro—but everyone knew there was only one Cathedral. The steps were perfect for Olivia to practice her walking.

On the north side was the *Municipalidad*. Downstairs was a museum of Antigua history. Upstairs were the offices where birth certificates were issued. As we strolled past, I realized that because we lived in Antigua, I could procure a copy of Olivia's original birth certificate, with Ana's name on it, which I could have never done from California. The "Delayed Record of Birth" issued by California eradicated any reference to Ana, naming only Tim and me as parents, which was only half the story. I was glad we would have a permanent record of Ana's essential contribution to our family.

We reached Fifth Avenida, where I saw the *Arco de Santa Catalina*, or "the Arch," stretching over the street. Back in the 1600s, cloistered nuns had used the Arch to cross from their convent to their garden without going outside. The tolling clock I had heard from our *casita* was added two hundred years later. Despite the early hour, painters were seated at their easels, rendering the Arch in misty pastels.

A few blocks over was Antigua's main grocery store, *La Bodegona*. Past that was the outdoor bus terminal, crowded with red and orange chicken buses, and the *mercado*, where tourists bought handicrafts we referred to as *típica* and locals bought almost anything else—from fruits and vegetables and raw beef hanging from hooks, to televisions, tube socks, and frilly white dresses for their daughters' First Holy Communion.

The shops on the Square's west side included a bookstore that stocked materials on contemporary Guatemalan artists. One of them, Óscar Perén, painted the interior of a chicken bus in its colorful, chaotic glory. A poster of Perén's picture hung in the bookstore window. If I could find the name of the museum that owned it, I'd go see the original canvas.

Police headquarters anchored the south side of the Square. Three young boys in uniform slouched against the wall, machine guns holstered at their sides. They reminded me of the boys in my high school English class, just beginning to shave. I lowered my head and walked by with a steady pace.

Few Guatemalans had Internet access in their homes, so Internet storefronts abounded. Conexión, where I was meeting Kendra, was on Fourth Calle East, down the street from Doña Luisa Bakery, famous for its orange chocolate bread and the whole-wheat loaf called *pan integral*.

Conexión was hard to find because the entrance was tucked in one corner of the Fuente Café, which was itself not easily seen. Like many businesses in Antigua, the Fuente Café was housed in a vast, former private residence dating from the colonial period. In these residences, the original double front doors had been built wide enough to accommodate a horse and buggy. A large central courtyard, paved in cobblestone and tile, always contained a fountain—a *fuente*.

I paused at the entrance, enchanted by the round tables covered with cloths the color of lime sherbet, the coffee-sipping couples, the classical music piped over speakers mounted in the creeping red bougainvillea. A white American woman with a Guatemalan baby strapped to her chest raised her arm to get my attention. Her full, tawny hair with strands of silver reminded me of a lion's mane. I wheeled the jogger over.

"You must be Jessica." She stood up and thrust out her hand. "I'm Kendra. We always stop for coffee first. I hope you don't mind."

She was six inches taller than I was, with the strong jaw and white teeth of someone born into affluence and good health—a testament to the benefits of protein. The veins on her muscled forearm stuck out like a relief map. She looked like she should be leading an expedition of adventure travelers in the steppes of Nepal.

"I can always drink more coffee," I said. "Olivia can always use more milk."

Kendra peeked into the jogger. The walk to Conexión had lulled Olivia to sleep. "She's a big girl," Kendra said.

"You don't want to know."

Kendra turned her shoulders to give me a better view of her sleeping baby. "This is Susanna. She's five months old."

"Look how tiny she is," I exclaimed. Susanna's head was no bigger than a grapefruit, but a distinctive beauty mark near her bottom lip made her appear precociously glamorous.

Kendra pulled out a chair. "Sit down. Join us."

A waitress walked over to the table with menus as I wheeled

Olivia beside the table and set the brake on the jogger. The waitress refilled Kendra's coffee cup and set a cup in front of me.

"*Café?*" she asked.

"*Por favor.*"

"Have you eaten?" Kendra opened her menu. "This will be my second breakfast, but who's counting?"

Kendra ordered the granola in the best Spanish I'd heard coming from an American. When I complimented her, she said she had learned it in the Peace Corps, twenty years ago, when she was stationed in the highland region. She spent four years in Guatemala then.

"Have you met any of the other moms yet?" Kendra asked. "Most of them can't count to ten in Spanish."

"Don't listen to my Spanish," I warned her.

"Stick around. You'll catch on."

Kendra stirred steamed milk into her coffee. "The other mothers are fine, actually, but they're typical Americans who get everything they want. Houses. Husbands. Babies. They live in Antigua, but can only talk about what they miss back home. Safe drinking water, cable TV, their cars. They're incredibly spoiled."

I appreciated safe drinking water as much as the next ugly American. But I also knew how destructive negativity was when allowed to feed on itself.

"Antigua isn't the first world," Kendra said. "But it's a lot better than the rest of Guatemala."

She moved her chair closer to mine, so close I saw yellow flecks in her green eyes. She seemed to be trying to look inside me—to decide if I was like the others. I wondered if Nadine had told her Tim was a physician. If Kendra was as practical as she appeared, that might have been reason enough to befriend me. I liked Kendra, and I wanted her to like me. She had lived here before; she knew the ropes. She spoke Spanish.

The waitress set down two heaping portions of granola, a dish of yogurt, and a dispenser of honey. She waited with hands on hips as Kendra surveyed the spread and pronounced it acceptable.

"Tell me about the Peace Corps," I said.

"I lived in one of the hardest hit villages in the civil war. Rabinal. I set up a program for the widows. Forty of them signed up; we could have signed up two hundred. They planted trees in exchange for a pound of beans or five pounds of corn. That's how they fed their children."

Kendra spooned yogurt over her granola and pushed the dish toward me. "I've never met anyone like those widows. Their husbands were dead, their kids starving, and for years the army stood on the border of their village with guns. Yet they were happy. Cheerful and joyous, even. The Americans could take a page from their book."

I stirred yogurt into my granola and took a few bites. "I always feel guilty when I hear stories like that," I said. "We have it so easy in the States."

Kendra picked up the dispenser of honey. "And yet still we complain," she said. She shrugged.

The key was to take Antigua on its own terms, Kendra said. Accept that it was different and make the best of it. Kendra urged me to buy a weekly pass to the swimming pool at Hotel Antigua. She and Susanna went every day. Also imperative was a gym membership. Working out kept Kendra sane. Last year, she had done Ironman Hawaii. The year before that, she climbed Mount Kilimanjaro.

"Kind of my last hurrah before motherhood," Kendra said. "I didn't want to have any regrets."

"I thought you looked fit," I said.

"You need to be strong to get through this," Kendra said. "You're pretty fit yourself. Nadine told me about your bike riding."

"Oh, well. I used to ride a lot more."

"Didn't we all," Kendra said.

Kendra suggested I hire a *niñera* to babysit so I could take Spanish classes. The classes were cheap and when else would I have such an opportunity? Taxicabs were not too expensive. Find a driver I trusted and use him exclusively. Kendra planned to tour the country with Susanna. They'd already spent a weekend at Lake Atitlán.

She shared with me the phone number for the best pediatrician in town and gave me names of good restaurants that served food safe to eat. Because she telecommuted in her job as a soil specialist, she knew the location of the only express mail and copy shop in Antigua, should the need ever arise.

"Is there anything you don't know?" I asked, jotting down notes.

"I don't know if I'll ever bring this little *chulita* home." Kendra kissed the top of Susanna's head. "That's one thing I don't know."

To hear her voice the doubt I felt was unnerving. I would never have said such a thing out loud.

Unlike Olivia and the other babies I'd met, Susanna had lived in an orphanage before Kendra moved down to live with her. Susanna's birth mother, Febi, had left her there when Susanna was two days old. It was a private orphanage with an excellent reputation, run by an American. But, said Kendra, it was still an orphanage. At night, they propped up the babies with bottles in their mouths so they wouldn't cry.

The orphanage director had warned Kendra the adoption could be difficult because Febi was only fifteen years old. Not only that, Febi had relinquished her first child as well. Cases involving mothers who had previously relinquished were scrutinized more closely by the U.S. Embassy and PGN. Febi had been thirteen the first time, but her mother, Susanna's grandmother, was alive then. The grandmother had since died.

"She either died in a car accident or was murdered," Kendra said. "I've heard both versions. We're waiting for the court to appoint her older sister as guardian."

I murmured a sympathetic comment.

"It could be worse. She could be an abandonment case, with no paperwork at all. Those take a year minimum." Kendra shook back her tawny hair. "One day at a time. I can handle it."

I had no doubt she could. Just by looking at her, I knew that Kendra was tough—you didn't climb Kilimanjaro and finish Ironman Hawaii if you were weak—and she expected everybody else to be tough, too. Best not to tell her about my near-breakdown my very first night alone with Olivia.

The waitress cleared our bowls and refilled our cups with coffee. Kendra stretched her arms over her head.

"If we were home in California, we'd be driving from one play-date to another," Kendra said. "Or sitting in a windowless office. Here, we can spend time with our kids."

"True enough," I said.

After we paid the bill, I roused Olivia and held her fingers as she toddled toward the fountain in the middle of the courtyard. Her footing was surer than I'd ever seen it. She was almost walking. Like the Cathedral steps, the grass around the fountain would be a good place for her to practice.

Kendra and Susanna came up behind us. "One more thing," Kendra said. "A lot of people here really don't like us."

"Because of adoption?"

"Way before that. When I was in the Peace Corps, I heard villagers say white people stole babies to harvest their organs. Or eat them. One woman insisted they sliced them open to transport drugs."

"Based on what?" I asked.

"Suspicion of outsiders. That and the civil war, which was believed to be backed by white people, namely the CIA. Rumors got started and they grew. Of course, the Guatemalan bureaucrats encouraged the suspicion. Better for them if the villagers hate an outside enemy. Takes the pressure off the bureaucrats."

Kendra unsnapped her baby carrier and placed Susanna on the grass. Susanna immediately fell over. Kendra bent over to set her upright.

"With adoption, the paranoia has gotten worse," Kendra said. "A few years ago, a tourist taking a picture was almost beaten to death because someone thought she was kidnapping a baby."

She gestured to the fountain, the creeping bougainvillea. "Don't be fooled by how tranquil everything seems. The Mayas fear us because we're foreigners. The bureaucrats hate us because we're adopting the Mayas, whom they also hate. Don't let your guard down for a minute."

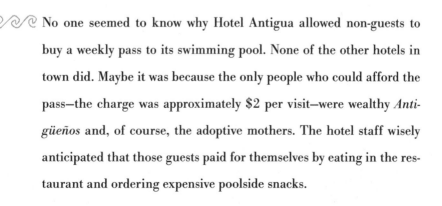 No one seemed to know why Hotel Antigua allowed non-guests to buy a weekly pass to its swimming pool. None of the other hotels in town did. Maybe it was because the only people who could afford the pass—the charge was approximately \$2 per visit—were wealthy *Antigüeños* and, of course, the adoptive mothers. The hotel staff wisely anticipated that those guests paid for themselves by eating in the restaurant and ordering expensive poolside snacks.

Even without the swimming pool, the hotel was splendid, a low-lying whitewashed structure built in the colonial style. Inside the court-yard, the fountain burbled. The high, vaulted ceiling recalled castles in Spain. The hotel's details honored Antigua's heritage: A collection of lacquered orange ceramic owls—Antigua's mascot—nestled in niches in the lobby. Tiles emblazoned with the city's crest—a man dressed in crimson astride a rearing horse—were laid in the floor of the entryway.

The swimming pool was encircled by gardens of pink and red hibiscus and shaded by palm trees. Olivia overcame her fear of water. The shallow end was low enough that she could walk with me beside her on my knees. When she tired of walking, she hung on the ladder and pulled herself up onto the deck to watch palm fronds spinning in the drain. The best part of the pool was that in it I could hold her without her resisting me. Sometimes I stood so long in the deep end she fell asleep in my arms.

One of the few play structures in Antigua was tucked in one corner of the lush, manicured lawn. More serviceable than deluxe, it consisted of two swings, a sandbox, and a slide. But, oh, how our children adored it! Olivia could spend an afternoon shoveling sand into a bucket or dripping handfuls of it over the bottom of the slide. She rarely made any sounds, which Tim had assured me was common for kids hearing two languages, but here she didn't need to. She sat hypnotized in a swing as I pushed her back and forth, back and forth, until my biceps burned.

Beside the play structure were two tall, narrow bird cages, home to the four resident parrots. During daylight hours, the parrots roosted high in the branches of an olive tree and squawked at the children below. The birds were native to the jungles in northern Guatemala, where the temperature was warmer and the air more steamy. As bucolic as Antigua is, it wasn't their natural habitat. Sometimes, as I watched them yammer and fuss, I was reminded of Olivia and me, living in a Garden of Eden, far from home.

On weekends, a marimba combo was stationed on one end of the pool deck, and their tinkling melodies filled the air. The musicians wore ruffled shirts and tight black pants with cummerbunds around their thickening middles. The first few times I walked by them with Olivia in my arms, I felt self-conscious, as though I had no right to carry a Guatemalan baby. But after a few weeks, we became accustomed to each other. When I passed the musicians, I lifted Olivia's hand to wave. They waved back.

On the other end of the pool deck, on Sundays, a craftswoman demonstrated weaving. One Sunday when I paused to watch, the craftswoman glanced up from her backstrap loom and a glimmer of recognition crossed her face. She pointed to Olivia and asked, "*Suya?*" shorthand for "Is she your daughter?"

"From Totonicapán," I said, my heart clutching. What if the craftswoman knew someone from Olivia's birth family, or even Ana herself? I considered digging deeper to find out if we had a connection, but fear held me back. Olivia wasn't officially ours, and I didn't want to do anything that might jeopardize that process. When the crafts-woman asked me the name of Olivia's *mamá biológica*, I shook my head as though I didn't understand the question.

I got to know most of the other adoptive mothers at the pool. Two of them, Mary Kay and Heather, came almost as regularly as Kendra and I did. Mary Kay had been in Antigua the longest—six months. Her year-old son, Joaquín, was her second Guatemalan adoption. Her older son lived back in Dallas with her husband, an investment banker with surfer-boy good looks. She was a classical pianist who missed her piano almost as much as she missed her husband and oldest son.

Heather had moved to Antigua a month before I did—beginning of July. She was only twenty-five, the youngest woman I'd ever met who was adopting. Heather had magenta hair and tattoos on each shoulder. Her husband was older than she was, an electrician with his own business outside of Denver, Colorado. They had shifted to Guatemala after they lost a referral when Vietnam shut down. Their daughter, Isabella, was the same age as Kendra's Susanna.

Two other women came once a month or so: Ruby and Catherine, a pediatrician and mother of ten, respectively. They kept to themselves and rarely ventured from their condos on the north side of town. I briefly knew others, too: an ICU nurse who lived in upstate New York; a special-ed teacher; a hairdresser from Tennessee.

But it was Kendra, Mary Kay, Heather, and I who became each

other's support group. Our children played together. We swapped kid-friendly menus, trip ideas, *notario* frustrations, restaurant recommendations. If one of us was having a bad day, the others propped her up. "We've all been there," was our mantra, whether that referred to a fussy child who could not be soothed, an impatient outburst we were ashamed to admit, or a husband on the end of a phone line who insisted we were on "vacation." We understood one another in a way no one else in the world seemed able to. Only we knew the late-night fear of losing a baby we loved.

Kendra had accused the women of being spoiled, but the longer I lived in Antigua, the more I came to believe the same could be said of any American. Our access to healthcare alone bestowed on us a privilege most Guatemalans could only dream of, not to mention our educational opportunities. I realized how advantaged we appeared as we unpacked our Dora the Explorer beach towels and fancy water wings. I cringed if one of us forgot to finish our lemonade and left it at the table beside a half-eaten hamburger. We had so much relative to everyone outside the walls of Hotel Antigua and beyond. We knew that.

Chapter 12

ANTIGUA

Finishing the adoption was harder than I thought. Not only was I not a Guatemalan *notario*, I wasn't even an American lawyer. The closest I'd come to legal training was working as a proofreader on the night shift at a corporate law firm in New York City. The fact that I spoke so little Spanish didn't help.

At first, I was still trying to get help from Yolanda.

"Has Ana signed yet?" I asked, referring to Guatemala's requirement that birth mothers sign their permission—or if they're illiterate, give a thumbprint—four different times. Ana had fulfilled two of those requirements: when she relinquished to the *notario*, Simón Guerrero, and at DNA. Two signatures remained, at the Family Court interview and at PGN.

"No signature," Yolanda responded. "*Notario* on vacation." She signed off with "SUICIDAL!" It was one of our last communications.

Theodore was equally useless. He'd stopped taking my phone

calls after Tim and I had dared to go to PGN and he had threatened me in the Camino Real elevator. I imagined him swaggering around the lobby in his Rolex watch, seeing my number flash on caller ID, and slipping his phone into his pocket, unanswered. I'd seen him do it a hundred times.

Our *notario*, Simón Guerrero, intimidated me—being locked in an office in downtown Guatemala City was not an experience I wished to relive, especially without Tim beside me—and I didn't have a number for his assistant, Gilda. I tried calling Señor Rodríguez to get the number from him, but I got lost in the PGN phone system.

I felt I had nowhere to turn.

On August 12, my second week in Antigua, I turned forty-five. Tim called and wished me a happy birthday. That weekend, in my honor, he was going on a long bike ride with our cycling group in Marin. He promised to eat a slice of chocolate cake, my favorite.

"I wish you were here to help me," I said.

"I wish I were, too," he said. "But I do have a job, remember?"

"I've got my hands full with Olivia, trying to be a good mom."

"We knew that before you left," said Tim. "Did you think it was going to get easy because it's your birthday?"

I didn't answer. A part of me *had* believed the adoption would somehow resolve itself once I moved to Antigua. Theodore would understand that I meant business. The *notario*, Simón Guerrero, and his assistant, Gilda, would see that I wasn't going away. Honestly, a part of me thought Yolanda would do the right thing and put pressure on all of them.

"Giving up isn't an option," Tim said before saying goodbye.

My birthday was a wake-up call. Whatever I was doing, it wasn't enough.

Our housekeeper, Paola, arrived every weekday morning at nine, and as soon as I heard her key in the lock, I loaded Olivia into the baby jogger for our morning stroll to Conexión to meet Kendra and check email. I had never had daily help in the house before, and it was impossible for me to play with Olivia or do anything else as long as Paola was working. I felt too guilty. Tim advised me to pretend I was a member of the upper crust, accustomed to ubiquitous yet invisible staff, but I knew myself better than that. It just wasn't going to happen.

Paola was mother to eight boys and one girl. That fact alone would seem to excuse her from performing any other duties. But no. To get to Antigua, she rode a chicken bus twenty miles from Chimaltenango, where her family slept in hammocks over a dirt floor that turned to mud during the six-month rainy season. Her day started before dawn, when she walked to and from the mill where she bought the corn meal required to make the one hundred and fifty tortillas her family ate every day, which she made herself, by hand.

How dare I complain about anything? Paola had finished a full day's work before I'd finished my first cup of coffee. She could hack a piece of firewood into a thousand shards of kindling with the aid of a simple kitchen knife, and knew how to light a fire using only one match. Compared to her, I was a pampered city girl who couldn't survive an overnight camping trip in a fully outfitted RV.

But Paola never said a word about how easy I had it. She scrubbed our bathroom and waxed the tile floor. She polished the dining room table and chairs and hung up the laundry. Paola had cleaned our *casita* for seventeen years. She paced herself as if looking toward another twenty.

I didn't know what Paola's husband did for a living. Paola accompanied any mention of him with a deep sigh. I got the impression Paola was teaching her sons to become better providers. Nevertheless, if Paola found as much as a *centavo* anywhere in the house, she left it on the dining room table so I could find it. Once, I had changed a stack of U.S. dollars into *quetzales* and, without thinking, stuffed the whole wad into the pocket of my blue jeans. The wad was still in my pocket when I threw the jeans into the laundry pile. Paola dried the sodden lump on the kitchen counter, every *quetzal* accounted for.

Watching Paola, I learned patience. At the beginning of the month, our bills for electricity and telephone were slipped through the mail slot by a delivery person. (There was no mail delivery in much of Guatemala.) The next day, Paola took the money I gave her, walked to the Square and queued up outside the banks with other

Antigüeños to pay for utilities. Two or three armed bank guards monitored each line. No one jostled or pushed; no one became irate or tried to cut in front of someone else. They simply waited, shoulder to shoulder, half the morning and sometimes until lunchtime.

Paola was not an effusive woman, but before we left on our morning stroll, she made a point of picking up Olivia to hug her, calling her *mi muñeca* and *la reina*. "My dolly" and "the queen." Near the end of August, our first month in the *casita*, Paola asked about the progress of our adoption. Keeping in mind her tolerance for delays, I explained adoptions were currently halted, and we had been involved in ours for more than a year. We had pre-approval from the American side and were trying to navigate the bureaucracies of Guatemala.

"They need to see your face," she said simply. "This close." She held up both her hands four inches apart as if they were talking to each other. "Then they understand."

She was absolutely right. Guatemala was a traditional country that valued personal relationships. Business was conducted face to face. In order for someone to help me, he had to first know who I was. Every Monday from then on, I took a cab into the capital to meet with Señor Rodríguez at PGN. He seemed to be in the position of most power. I decided he was our best hope.

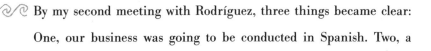 By my second meeting with Rodríguez, three things became clear: One, our business was going to be conducted in Spanish. Two, a

translator might not always be available. Three, I was never sure that the translator was accurately communicating my concerns.

I needed to learn Spanish. To do so, I needed someone to take care of Olivia for a few hours every week.

Kendra gave me the name of her *niñera's* sister. Aracely was in her late thirties and mother to five children, ages five to sixteen. When she stopped by for an interview, she clapped her hands and opened her arms wide to Olivia. Olivia reached for her as though they'd known each other forever. On Aracely's third day, she showed up with her son, Junior, in tow. Five years old, he was as sweet and energetic as a puppy. He greeted Olivia by slapping his open palm to his forehead and bobbling his head with the impact. Olivia responded with a sound so unfamiliar, I almost didn't recognize it.

"Is that a *giggle?*" I put my ear up to Olivia's mouth. "I think it is."

As concerned as I was with Olivia's adoption, I had forgotten to consider how isolated she must have felt with only me after the hubbub of the Garza family. Undoubtedly, she missed them as much as I missed Tim. When I watched her spin around the living room, laughing with Junior, I felt a twinge of sadness. If only I had finished the adoption within six months, or at least moved to Antigua sooner, Olivia's separation from Lupe might not have been so difficult.

I hugged Olivia goodbye, relieved I was leaving her in such capable hands. As I hurried to class, I debated whether I should invite

Lupe to visit or if such a reunion might further confuse Olivia. There was no map for the road on which we were traveling.

The first Spanish class I signed up for was conducted in a grass hut. It offered no books or paper; the curriculum was free-form. The teacher, Gladys, and I sat knee to knee on two small chairs while Gladys asked me questions in Spanish: *What work does your husband do? How much money does he make? Don't you want to have your own child?*

I felt as if I were undergoing an interrogation to which I responded with the same thirty or forty words. I believed in the total immersion method, but I knew that I needed more structure; a list of vocabulary also would have helped.

Nadine, whom I sometimes ran into at Conexión, suggested the Christian Spanish Academy, a school founded for the hundreds of evangelical missionaries who were posted every year in Guatemala and throughout Central and South America. The Academy's curriculum was more structured than at other schools, which was a better fit for the way I learned. Not only did it utilize vocabulary lists, white boards and markers, it printed its own series of textbooks, ranging from *Grado A* to *Grado G*.

The first day, I took an assessment test which placed me in *Grado A*. There I remained (alas) for my entire enrollment.

My teacher, Lila, and I were the lone Catholics among the evangelical missionaries—friendly, freckle-faced youngsters from places like Missouri and Utah and Alabama. They took classes for four hours every morning and two hours in the afternoon. Within a few short weeks, I heard them conversing more fluently than I ever had.

The teachers were mostly married women who had graduated from high school, which placed them in Guatemala's privileged class. Dressed in tidy white blouses, blue trousers, and vests monogrammed with the school's initials, they looked like well-heeled society matrons compared to us scruffy Americans. Lessons were conducted at small square tables around an open courtyard. On rainy afternoons—which meant most of them—my teacher Lila and I huddled at our table shielded by our white board and watched sheets of rain pound down from the sky. I learned the words *lluvia*—rain—and *paraguas*—umbrella—although nobody in Antigua seemed to use *paraguas*, wisely opting to wait out deluges crouched in a doorway or under an overhang.

Lila was twenty-nine years old and lived with her parents. Most of our conversations centered on how she yearned to get married. Many times I had to repeat the story of how I had met Tim on a four-hundred-mile, five-day bike ride. I had lived in San Diego; Tim in San Francisco. For a year, we had dated long distance. He sent me homemade bread through the mail.

Lila related details of her crush on a boy she referred to as *el chico*. On Tuesday and Thursday evenings, he rode his bicycle to her house and visited with Lila and one of her sisters. One Monday afternoon, after a weekend festival in their town, Lila was radiant as she told me that she and *el chico* had actually danced a single dance together. Not the salsa, she assured me, as if to say she was not "that kind of girl," but the merengue, a courtlier dance that implied his serious intentions.

Despite our shared hopes and the promising detail of the bicycle, the relationship never developed. After weeks of listening to the saga, I decided *el chico* was either more interested in Lila's sister than in Lila or not interested in women at all. Perhaps he was destined for the priesthood.

"*Basta!*" I begged. "Enough!"

I couldn't bear to watch Lila pine for an unavailable man while her life passed by. I wanted her to see herself for the attractive, smart woman she was. At first, I urged her to join an exchange program to improve her English in the United States, or at least widen her horizons by working in Guatemala City. But her world was Antigua, her family, and her church, and her dream remained the dream of that boy getting off his bicycle and sitting down to stay.

Chapter 13

FAMILY COURT

September 4: day thirty-five in Antigua. Olivia was fifteen months old.

Tim and my family stopped asking when I was coming home. Instead, they reported on connections they had and leads they were following. We were looking for anyone with any sort of governmental power in the off chance they could help. My sister Adrienne's girlhood pal was an ambassador in the Middle East. Tim's office assistant knew someone in our state senator's office. I queried the president of an international coffee company, headquartered in Guatemala, whose niece was a patient of Tim's.

Each response was the same: Sorry. No. Wish we could help.

My sister, Patrice, called with news. Her old boyfriend had a friend married to a Guatemalan woman. Teresa came from a wealthy, educated family who owned language schools throughout Central America. She spoke English flawlessly. The most amazing part of Teresa's story was that she and her American husband, Jack, had adopted a thirteen-year-old Guatemalan boy, Lucas, when he was eight. At age six, he had wandered into the Guatemala City orphanage where Teresa volunteered, the only one in his family to survive a military raid on his village.

Somehow, I knew she would help me. I called and explained our situation. I had made a friend at PGN, Señor Rodríguez. He promised to assist me, but he could not do anything until our case was submitted to PGN from Family Court. The problem was that I didn't know if our case was *in* Family Court. Teresa said, "Arrange for your *niñera*. We're going to Family Court to investigate."

"Even for us, adoption was difficult," Teresa said the following morning, as we bumped over the cobblestones in her black SUV. The windows were so darkly tinted I could barely see Olivia at the curb, waving goodbye from Aracely's arms.

Teresa had driven in from the capital to pick me up. She was thirty-five, apple-cheeked and curvy, with short, corkscrew hair and merry eyes. A gold wedding band and a Timex watch were her only jewelry. Her white polo reminded me of California. I liked her immediately.

Teresa continued: "Lucas was an abandonment, with no birth certificate, no family. No birth mother to give her signature. The social worker in Family Court could not write her report without this information. It took almost two years."

I stared at her in the driver's seat, stunned by the good fortune of having met her. Only a minute percentage of Guatemalans legally adopted children, and fewer still were English-speaking Ladinos who adopted Mayas. I had heard one statistic that stated only ten such cases were completed each year, and the person who told me the number believed it was exaggerated.

"How did you finally succeed?" I asked.

"The second year, we went in before Christmas with a bottle of wine and good chocolate. Lucas was ours after New Year's." Teresa shifted gears to climb the hill out of Antigua. "This was the only way."

Family Court was housed in the Supreme Court of Justice building in the central plaza of Guatemala City's Civic Center. National banks and high-rise office buildings surrounded the plaza on all sides. Men in business suits crisscrossed the plaza carrying briefcases. Women in high heels and dressy pants strode among them, cell phones to their ears. Looking out the window from the passenger seat in Teresa's SUV, I dared to hope that we were finally, *finally*, entering the place where decisions were made.

Teresa parked in an attended lot two blocks from the courthouse. She opened the window less than an inch to accept the ticket from the attendant. Before we got out of the car, she showed me how to carry my pocketbook: close to my body on the inside, not on the sidewalk side. She pointed to the waistband of my pants and instructed me to hide my passport.

I tucked it in as demonstrated. "Are you afraid I'll lose it?"

"I'm afraid someone will stick a gun in your face and steal it." She unbuckled her seatbelt and waited for me to do the same. "Follow me and run fast so nobody catches us."

The wide stone staircase that led into the court building was so steep I felt as if I were scaling the side of a pyramid. We passed through a security checkpoint, and I watched in disbelief as everyone but us pulled a handgun out of his pocket and checked it with the attendant. Later, Teresa informed me that with enough money it was easy to procure a handgun license in Guatemala.

Inside, my eyes adjusted. Bland oatmeal-color walls melded into a dingy marble floor. Office workers lined up at a snack bar waiting for coffee. A *muchacha* with a basket on her head walked the length of the line, selling tortillas. The primary light source seemed to be from the illuminated numbers above the two elevators. Except for the tortillas and coffee, I could have been in the DMV office back home in California, circa 1972.

Every adoption was assigned a case number. On the way downtown, Teresa had called our *notario*, Simón Guerrero, to ask for ours, but he refused to give it to her. He did, however, reveal that we were assigned to Court One. This information was more valuable than I'd realized because the building had nine floors of courtrooms and no information desk.

Court One was on the first floor, across from the security check-point and behind the snack bar. As I waited for Teresa to introduce herself to the desk clerk, I smelled the roasting coffee beans and heard peppers and onions sizzling in oil. I read a sign over the doorway to Court One that declared only lawyers and those with court business were permitted to enter.

The desk clerk asked Teresa if either one of us was a lawyer.

"*Americana,*" Teresa said, as if the two were synonymous. She launched into a lengthy explanation into which she injected multiple references to Tim's last name, Berger. Without directly saying so, she implied that the likely next president of Guatemala was a distant relation of my husband's. The clerk harrumphed. Without our case number, she couldn't tell us if our case was registered or not. But she wouldn't stop us if we wanted to look for ourselves.

Court One wasn't a courtroom in the conventional sense, but a rabbit warren of social workers' offices. I followed Teresa through the labyrinth. Through the open office doors I saw green metal filing cabinets and desks overflowing with manila folders. I was careful not to make eye contact with anyone lest they try to stop us.

At the end of a narrow hallway, we came to a library. Long tubes of fluorescent lights hummed overhead. Floor to ceiling bookcases chock full of leather- and cloth-bound volumes the size of high-school yearbooks lined the walls and filled the room's interior. Teresa went straight to three shelves in the middle of the room filled with identical light gray, cloth-covered volumes.

"You've done this before," I said.

She nodded.

The section heading read "*Adopción*." Just seeing the word made me choke up.

Teresa made the sign of the cross and said in Spanish, "It's before God." She reached to the middle shelf and pulled down a ledger marked on the spine, January through June 2002. She handed it to me, and I carried the book to a table in the corner and made my own tight sign of the cross.

As had been the case in PGN, every single record was handwritten, in a consistent, slanting penmanship. Once again, I was struck by how labor-intensive the process was. Someone had to draw in the columns with a red pen and ruler and handwrite every name. In the Camino Real, I had sometimes heard Theodore tell families that Family Court information wasn't available because it was "at the bindery." As I held the cloth-bound ledger in my hands, I realized he may have been telling the truth.

Because I didn't know our case number, I started from May 20, the day Olivia was born. I dragged my index finger down the page, searching for Ana's name. I tried to read every syllable, but I was so eager to find Ana, I began to skim the columns. Twenty minutes passed. I had made it to June 2002, with no luck. I closed the ledger and returned it to the shelf before selecting another. July 2002 through December 2002. I carried the book to the table and continued the process. Midway through September 2002, I noticed Teresa had moved to a corner with her ledger and was sitting cross-legged on the floor. I picked up my book and sank to the floor, too.

The desk clerk appeared at the doorway, inquiring how much longer we planned to stay. It was one o'clock and the office closed at three. Teresa scrambled to her feet to express her gratitude. The clerk looked at me on the floor and I lowered my head, proud that I may have been the only American who had made it this far into Family Court. I said a prayer thanking God for Teresa. The clerk withdrew and disappeared through the rabbit warren. Teresa winked and gave me a thumbs-up.

Teresa and I had scanned every listing through June 2003, the last bound volume available. My legs were numb from sitting with them folded. I desperately needed to go to the bathroom. I was worried that Simón Guerrero and his assistant, Gilda, had never submitted the case to Family Court after we received Embassy pre-approval.

Teresa said we needed to start over and read each name more deliberately. She understood that I was eager to find our case, but I must not hurry.

I opened the volume for January through May 2003 and began again. I said aloud each name registered in January, February, and March. I reached the month of April. I read through April 10.

April 11, 2003.

Ana Herlinda Xoc Toledo. Case number 9147. Simón Guerrero, *Notario.*

I was unsure if I was seeing Ana's name or only imagining it. I underlined her name with my fingernail. A lump rose in my throat.

My voice cracked as I called out the news to Teresa.

She scooted over to where I was sitting and I pointed to the entry on the page. We leaned into each other and hugged so hard the book started to close on my lap. Teresa thrust her hand into the pages, marking the place. Tears ran down my face, and I pulled away from her, embarrassed to be blubbering in front of someone I barely knew.

Teresa passed me a tissue. "*You* found it. That's a good sign."

I blew my nose. Teresa jotted down our case number. Seeing Ana's name recorded in an official book meant that the government of Guatemala recognized our case.

The adoption was started in both countries. Someday, somehow, I would finish it.

After I determined our case was in Family Court, my mission became to move it to step four, into PGN. To do so, Ana needed to come into the capital to be interviewed by a social worker and sign her permission, the third of her fourth required signatures. The case had been in Family Court for four months and so far the signature hadn't happened. During my next Monday meeting, I turned to Señor Rodríguez.

"It's Theodore's job to pick up Ana," I said. "He still won't take my calls."

Rodríguez pressed the button on his speaker phone. "*G-i-i-i-l-da!*" he screamed when the *notario*'s assistant answered. "Go to Toto and find Ana!"

He promised to call me as soon as Ana's interview was done. Gilda would be the one who submitted the case to PGN. She was more cooperative than the *notario*. Once it was in PGN, he assured me, he would shepherd the case himself.

"*No te preocupes*, Jessie," he said. "Don't worry."

The next morning, I sat at the edge of the shallow end of the pool, watching Olivia poke her finger in the middle of the drain cover on the pool deck. Kendra and Heather were there with their girls, napping on blankets under umbrellas. Mary Kay held Joaquín on her lap. Three days ago, he'd spiked a fever, which had finally broken. This was their first day out of the house.

"We're almost out of Family Court," I said. I didn't mention Rodríguez's role; I rarely did. Each of us was working our own angles, and we didn't always divulge what they were. "Next step, PGN."

"The four signatures are a pain," said Mary Kay. "We wasted three months in Family Court during our first adoption. The birth mother couldn't take off from her factory job. For this one, we had her sign her own power of attorney in the very beginning. The *notario* is signing for her."

"Those *notarios* think of everything," said Kendra.

"I thought the four signatures were so she'd have four opportunities to change her mind," I said.

"She can't change her mind." Mary Kay laid her palm across Joaquín's forehead. "Not if she's been paid. How would she pay back the money?"

I glanced over at Olivia, playing at the drain cover. "Is that true?" Nikki at the Camino Real had said the same thing, but I hadn't believed it then, either. "Are they really paid?"

"Some of them are," said Mary Kay. "Not a lot, but definitely paid."

Heather frowned. "Big frigging deal. That goes on in the States, too. I knew someone who bought her birth mother a car, sent her to Disneyland, and rented her an apartment for six of the nine months. How is it different?"

"Money means more here," said Kendra. "Most people make less than four bucks a day."

"How many of them are paid?" I said. "All of them? Half? One a year?"

"Some," said Mary Kay. "Let's face it. There are expenses involved in being pregnant, plus coming in for the signatures. The ones who are making the money are the *buscadoras*. I heard they get $5,000 for a baby girl. The birth mothers get a few hundred at most."

"Well that sucks," said Heather. "If anyone gets money, it should be the birth mother. I say give them more."

"I don't understand why they don't regulate it," Mary Kay said.

"License the *buscadoras* and *notarios* and if they get out of control, yank the license. It seems so obvious."

"It was the same in Vietnam," said Heather. "A bunch of money-grubbing lowlifes got involved. They'll shut down Guatemala, and some other country will become the hot new place. Brazil. Tibet. Ethiopia."

"I'm so sick of all of it," said Mary Kay. "My four-year-old at home refuses to go to preschool. My husband's so irate he can't talk to me. I'm exhausted. You don't know what it's like to have a kid with a 103 temperature and not know what to do. I'll do anything to get out of here."

"Why didn't you call my pediatrician?" Kendra asked.

"I gave him baby Tylenol. But I was still nervous."

The little girls started moving on their blankets, whimpering for their mothers. Olivia walked toward me, tired of the game around the drain. Joaquín sat up in Mary Kay's arms, seeming more awake and looking for action.

I turned to Kendra. "Do you think birth mothers are getting paid?"

She reached over to scratch Susanna's back. "What if they are? I'm the last person to judge any woman for her personal decisions. All over the world, every day, women give up their kids. Each one for a different reason. It's the *buscadoras* I object to. They're like fishing boats who've over-fished one area of the ocean. They have to cast their nets wider and use better bait."

Mary Kay stood up. "This little guy and his brother would be living on the street if we hadn't adopted them. Their father's a gangbanger." She took her son's hand. "Come on, Joaquín. Let's go swimming."

Kendra looked at me and raised her eyebrows. Mary Kay had been in Guatemala too long. She couldn't say the word "Hague" without breaking down.

Olivia pulled the backpack from the carriage underneath the jogger. She knew that was where I stored the snacks. As I watched her, I thought about asking Yolanda outright whether she'd paid Ana. But Yolanda had put her own daughter in an orphanage because foster care was too expensive. She hadn't paid Lupe. I couldn't imagine that she'd offered money to Ana.

September 22: day fifty-three. By my eighth week in Antigua, my gray roots were an inch long. My blonde tint had faded to the color of mouse fur, and in a forty-five-year-old woman, that was not a good look. I needed a colorist.

Kendra was my go-to person for all things Guatemalan, but I couldn't ask her; I was too embarrassed to reveal my vanity. Heather's magenta, I assumed, came out of a bottle. Which left Mary Kay. When I ran into her at the pool, she gave me the cell phone number of her stylist. Unfortunately, Belli at "Kinky Afro" was so popular that she was booked until mid-November. I decided to pick a place at random.

I packed Olivia into the jogger and we wandered for a few

blocks until I saw a *salón de belleza* with a hand-lettered sign that read "Irma's." Posters of Farrah Fawcett look-alikes and men sporting Glen Campbell sideburns festooned the front window. Perhaps I should have turned away, but I went in. A middle-aged woman in a green print housedress topped with a white frilly apron sat at a small desk beside the front door. She was eating tortillas while watching a portable color TV with rabbit ears fashioned from a wire hanger.

I looked past her to see a single folding metal chair in front of a cracked mirror. Beyond that was a white ceramic sink beside a green curtain. We were the only people there.

"*Qué linda!*" Irma said of Olivia. She wiped her mouth on the corner of her apron and pushed herself up from her chair. "*Qué alegre!*"

I was so grateful to hear Irma call Olivia "cute" and "happy" that I decided to entrust my hair to her on the spot.

"*Es posible, rubio?*" I removed the baseball cap I was wearing to cover my roots. "Blonde, like this?"

Irma disappeared behind the green curtain. I wheeled the jogger into the salon and positioned Olivia in front of the television set, as far away as possible from hair-coloring chemicals. I had worried that Olivia would create mischief by opening drawers and pulling out scissors and clips, but the only supplies I saw on the tray beside the folding chair were a black plastic Ace comb, a kitchen timer, and a rusted can of Aqua Net hair spray. Besides, Olivia was mesmerized by what looked to be a Guatemalan version of *Wheel of Fortune*.

I sat on the folding chair.

Irma reappeared, stirring a bowl of white foam that smelled like straight Clorox. She placed the concoction on the tray next to the Aqua Net and tucked a white dishtowel around the neckline of my T-shirt. The hairs inside my nose bristled.

I had expected Irma to apply the color with a stiff brush and wrap the treated strands into squares of aluminum foil. That was what my stylist back home did—methodically from front to back. Instead, Irma dropped three heaping tablespoons of white goop onto my head and sudsed it up with her bare fingers. I felt my scalp begin to burn. Getting blonde highlights in a country where most of the population was brunette might not have been a good idea.

Irma pulled a pink shower cap from her apron pocket and tucked the whole foamy mess inside. She wiped her hands on her apron and set the timer. *"Cuarenta y cinco minutos."*

Forty-five minutes. My stylist never let me go longer than thirty, tops, but I didn't want to appear pushy. I only hoped my scalp could tolerate it.

Irma lumbered over to open the front door and air out the room. I stayed back, not wanting to get too close to Olivia with my toxic head. I tried to distract myself from the burning sensation by pressing my hands together as hard as I could. In less than ten minutes, I couldn't stand it. *"Caliente!"* I called out. *"Tengo calor!"*

Irma hustled me by the arm to the sink, dragging over the

folding chair with us. When she removed the shower cap, my sinuses cleared as if I had swallowed wasabi. She told me to move the chair beside the sink and lean my head over. I arched my back and braced my feet on the linoleum tile so I wouldn't slip. I waited for the sound of water whooshing through a thick plastic hose for the final rinse.

Instead, I heard a faucet turn on. The swish of water filling a small plastic cup.

I felt the dribble of cold water on my forehead, the narrow teeth of the comb pressing at the roots.

Irma instructed me to flip over and dangle my head under the faucet so she could approach from that angle. With my knee on the chair, I watched the foam slide slowly down the sink.

My hair was pure yellow, bone-dry straw. The only solution was to cut it off, and I asked Irma to oblige. In a whirlwind of scissor snips, she sheared off most of the hair she had just colored, leaving me looking like Andy Warhol. Irma tried to refuse payment, but I insisted, folding in an extra twenty *quetzales*. I hugged her before we left.

Once I got used to it, the close crop was quite flattering. The other moms told me I looked ten years younger.

 Kendra read me the announcement as we both checked email at Conexión on October 6. The Guatemalan Congress had declared that imposing the requirements of the Hague Treaty on adoptions was unconstitutional. PGN, and not a Central Authority, would continue to oversee the process. The two of us twirled around in our seats in jubilation. We celebrated by logging off and heading straight for the Fuente Café for a second breakfast, giant stacks of pancakes smothered in maple syrup, much to the sugary delight of Olivia and Susanna. We toasted each other with glasses of fresh-squeezed orange juice and cups of coffee.

The next day, I left Olivia with Aracely and Junior and took a cab into the capital to meet Señor Rodríguez. He clasped my right hand between both of his in a warm handshake and hurried me into his office. "Your hair is different," he said. "*Rubio.*"

His mouth dropped open when I told him that I had found my way into Family Court with the help of Teresa. I told him I had missed Ana's name the first time I looked, but found it the second.

"Jessie," he said, shaking his wrist *Ay, ay, ay* and grinning. "*Eres valiente y fuerte.*" "You are brave and strong."

I blushed at the compliment. "*Gracias, señor.*"

"*Por favor*, Jessie." He tilted his head so he could see into my face. "Call me Miguel."

I looked up sharply. Although we were about the same age, I had always addressed him as Señor Rodríguez and used the formal pronoun, "*usted.*" I didn't want to offend him, but I didn't want to call him Miguel, either.

I walked over to the sofa and took my usual spot. Rodríguez

pushed his bangs back on his forehead as he sat in his desk chair. The room was silent for a long moment.

Rodríguez cleared his throat. For the record, he wanted me to know that he approved of my living in Antigua with Olivia. However, other people in PGN—he wouldn't name names—were not so pleased with the arrangement. PGN had appointed Lupe as Olivia's foster mother, not me. I had no legal right to keep her with me.

When I heard the words "no legal right to keep her," perspiration broke out under my arms. I had no one to blame but myself for exposing us to this level of scrutiny. We were simply too visible. "Does this mean you're going to take her away?" My voice was steady. I was already formulating a plan about how I could hide her with Aracely.

Señor Rodríguez stood up and walked around the edge of his desk. When he put his right hand on my shoulder, I stared at the floor. I had no idea how to interpret his actions. I only knew that he had the authority to let Olivia stay with me or take her away.

He squeezed my shoulder once before letting his hand drop. He walked back around his desk and sank into his chair. "You will need special paperwork."

The paper required Ana's permission and signature. Señor Rodríguez would call Simón Guerrero's assistant, Gilda, to make the arrangements. I nodded to show I agreed. My breathing was shallow and jagged.

Any interaction with Ana could result in her rethinking her

decision to relinquish. Any interaction with Gilda could take weeks to expedite. The best I could hope was that Señor Rodríguez would allow me to keep Olivia in the meantime. I concentrated on breathing.

Rodríguez opened one of two dozen manila folders on his desk, and I recognized our dossier. Upside down, I saw the photographs I had submitted two years earlier: Me in my wedding dress, Tim in his good blue suit, our house in Marin, our garden. We looked so young and innocent. I had selected the images painstakingly, hoping to convey our worthiness as parents. But here in Rodríguez's office, I viewed them through his eyes and they seemed only to show how naive we were.

He studied the photos for a long time and finally turned the page.

"Your daughter was placed with another foster mother before Lupe Garza," he said. "Griselda Chávez. Your daughter lived with her for four months."

He pulled a paper from the manila folder and pushed it toward me.

The official document stamped by PGN named Griselda Chávez as Olivia's legal foster mother. Yolanda had indicated Olivia was placed with Lupe at birth. Lupe acted as though she'd always had Olivia. Who the hell was Griselda Chávez?

Rodríguez passed me a Post-it and a pen so I could write down Griselda's address. "You can keep your baby until we get this straightened out. I'll call Gilda for the signature."

"*Gracias, señor.*"

We both knew I would never call him Miguel.

I wasn't sure if I would knock on Griselda's door to introduce myself. I just wanted to see where Olivia had lived for the first four months of her life. If it was an orphanage, I would knock. If it was a private residence, I would decide when we got there.

My cab driver, Juan Carlos, waited for me behind the wheel of his car, reading the morning edition of *El Diario*. I handed him Griselda's address. "Can you drive me?"

Juan Carlos handed the address back to me. "No," he said. "That neighborhood is Febrero Fourth in Zone 7. Too dangerous."

Neighborhoods in Guatemala City were sometimes named after notorious dates. Febrero Fourth had been founded by squatters in 1975 on the day of the great earthquake that took fifty thousand lives.

"How bad can it be?" I hadn't seen a Guatemala City neighborhood yet that wasn't defined by razor wire fences and men carrying submachine guns.

"The police don't go in that neighborhood unless there are three hundred of them. Every one of them armed. That neighborhood is filled with drugs, ruled by gangs." He shook his head emphatically. "We can't go there."

I gripped the back of his seat with my fingers. "We have to go."

"In Zone 7, if you leave your window open and we're waiting at a stoplight, they'll steal the sunglasses off your face."

"I'll keep the window rolled up."

"They can drag you out of the car and hold you for ransom."

"I'll keep the doors locked."

Juan Carlos turned the key in the ignition and pressed the gas pedal to the floor. "As you wish, señora."

I fastened my seat belt as he gunned the car north.

"These aren't real houses they live in. They took the property from the city." Juan Carlos addressed me in his rearview mirror. "There's no roads, only dirt paths. If there's a fire, too bad. The fire department won't go in. The people burn up."

I reached for the strap above my door as the car veered around the cloverleaf on Boulevard Liberación. "Tell me when I need to roll up my window."

"You'll know."

As we continued north, the road became dustier and more pot-holed. Piles of trash were heaped on both sides. We crossed a small stream into Zone 7. I peered through my closed window to see clusters of ramshackle huts collapsing against each other high in the hills.

The car lurched off the main road. Gravel crackled under the tires. Febrero Fourth looked like a shantytown in a bombed-out war zone. Small fires burned on pathways between the houses. Mangy dogs wandered loose and uncollared. I braced myself for the sound of gunfire.

A young man dressed in baggy jeans lounged against the front door of the shack closest to us. Even with my window closed, I could hear *ranchero* music blasting from the radio beside him. He turned his head toward us and spat, his hands in his pockets. "You want to talk to him?" Juan Carlos asked.

I stared out the window. Olivia had lived here for four months until Tim and I visited for the first time. If not for that visit, Yolanda might have left her here forever.

How could she have done that to a baby? Alone in her crib, seeing and hearing God knows what. Terrified. No wonder she had been so freaked out in our hotel room. She didn't know who we were or where we were taking her. No wonder she had clung to Lupe.

I wanted to kill Yolanda. She was willing to sacrifice our daughter's safety to save money. How many other children had she placed here? Foster mothers probably didn't charge much in Febrero Fourth.

"Yes or no?" Juan Carlos said. "Stay or go?"

Before I could answer, he threw the car into reverse, and we backed out in a cloud of dirt and rocks. We didn't even get to Griselda's shack. I had seen enough.

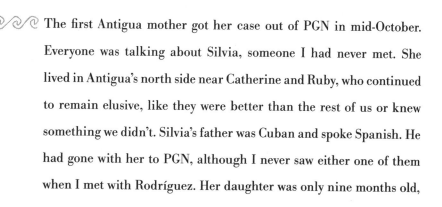 The first Antigua mother got her case out of PGN in mid-October. Everyone was talking about Silvia, someone I had never met. She lived in Antigua's north side near Catherine and Ruby, who continued to remain elusive, like they were better than the rest of us or knew something we didn't. Silvia's father was Cuban and spoke Spanish. He had gone with her to PGN, although I never saw either one of them when I met with Rodríguez. Her daughter was only nine months old,

which seemed unfair. Not that Silvia didn't deserve to get out—she did—but in my opinion, those of us with children who had celebrated their first birthdays in Guatemala deserved to get out more.

Still, Silvia's PGN victory meant there was hope for all of us. Kendra and I celebrated after dinner with macadamia nut pie at Cinderella Bakery on Fifth Avenida. The two of us rarely ate macadamia nut pie because it was a cholesterol bomb, and we never met at night because of our babies' bedtime schedules. But the first case getting out of PGN—even if it wasn't ours—was an event so auspicious we needed to honor it.

Because of Guatemala's position near the equator, the sun went down year-round at six o'clock, so by the time we had finished our pie and cleaned up the mess wreaked by Olivia and Susanna, it was very dark outside. Olivia and I lived diagonally across the Square; it seemed silly to hire a cab to drive us home. Kendra lived quite a bit farther south and west, past Hotel Antigua, but she didn't hire one, either. I pushed Olivia in the jogger. Kendra carried Susanna in her front-pack.

As Kendra left us off at our front door and headed into the darkness, I gave her my flashlight. "There aren't any streetlights. Are you sure you'll be safe?"

Kendra assured me she would.

When Kendra told me about the incident the next day, she tried to laugh it off. The guy was a punk, she said, and not a very smart one. Of all the Americans he could have chosen to tangle with, he picked the one who climbed Kilimanjaro. He attacked from behind, wrestling her to the ground. She kicked herself free before managing to stand up and run. The man disappeared into the shadows.

But I could tell she was spooked. Not because of herself, but because of what could have happened to Susanna. She didn't so much as bump her head, thank God, but it could have been bad. Neither Kendra nor I needed to verbalize how bad it could have been. We made a pact not to go out after dark unless absolutely necessary. If we had to, we promised each other we would hire a taxi.

I didn't tell Tim or my family about the incident. Although Señor Rodríguez had called me *valiente* and *fuerte*, they knew me better as someone afraid to go downstairs to our basement unless Tim came with me, a person who checked the locks on every window and door before going to bed. I didn't want them to worry.

 For a couple of weeks, Tim had been telling me I needed to extend my ninety-day tourist visa before it expired. I kept putting it off, because in order to get a new one, I needed to leave the country. I could take a bus and cross the border into Honduras or El Salvador, but I didn't want to risk not being let back across the border. And what would I do with Olivia? Tim wasn't going to arrive until Thanksgiving, and I didn't want to subject her to a reunion with the Garzas because that would require another separation. Kendra and Aracely offered to help, but I just couldn't bear the thought of Olivia going to bed not knowing where I was.

Kendra told me about an American named Millicent who could take care of it for $40 in *quetzales*. When she returned your passport after a week, it was stamped and official. You could stay another ninety days. The rule, I knew, was that you never, ever gave your passport to anyone. But I couldn't chance showing up at Immigration with an expired passport stamp when I finally returned home with Olivia. I had to trust Millicent.

Millicent lived north of us on Fourth Avenida on the way to the Square. Her house took up half a block, with a wooden door so large it looked as if it were designed for a medieval castle. I felt like a child when I stood on tiptoe to reach the brass doorknocker.

Millicent answered the door blocking the sun with her forearm. She was dressed in a housecoat and black cardigan and white terrycloth slippers. Her champagne blonde wig had slipped slightly to one side.

"You found me," she croaked in a thin voice. "Watch your step over the threshold." Her pale, grayish skin hung in crepey folds over her sunken cheeks. Her teeth—the ones that weren't missing—were faintly green.

I stepped over the wooden threshold into the courtyard, which was so cluttered with junk that I couldn't tell where the outside space ended and the interior of the house began. Rusted wagon wheels, chipped pottery, faded paintings, piles of moldy textiles. Millicent may have been the only owner of a grand Antigua residence who didn't employ a housekeeper.

She led me to a tiny, dark office at the end of the courtyard.

"My son, Toño, does the actual passport work." She gestured to a framed picture on her desk of a dark-skinned man whose features looked chiseled from stone.

Millicent must have noticed my puzzled expression because she added, "He's not really my son, but I call him that. He can fix anything."

I turned the frame toward me for a closer look.

"He's Kaqchikel Indian," Millicent said. "The indigenous are the smartest people in this country, and don't let anyone tell you otherwise."

I nodded in agreement. I only hoped Toño was more organized than Millicent appeared to be, or I would be living in Guatemala illegally, forever.

Millicent adjusted her wig. "How many weeks do you have left?" she asked. She plucked a pair of reading glasses from her desk drawer and set them on her nose.

I unfolded my passport and laid it in front of her.

She held the passport at arm's length to inspect it. "We had to extend another American eight times," she said. "The lady lived here two years."

"My daughter's almost eighteen months old," I said.

Millicent drew in her breath, making a whistling sound through the gaps in her teeth. "She in an orphanage?"

"Foster care. But she's with me now."

Millicent paper-clipped my *quetzales* to the first page of my passport, then opened a shoebox on her desk and placed the document inside. I was a little amazed at my willingness to turn over my passport to a complete stranger I knew virtually nothing about and wondered how difficult it would be to procure a replacement. Easier than taking a bus to Honduras, I hoped.

"What brought you to Guatemala?" I asked.

"Forty years ago my husband was in the diplomatic corps. But he's long gone."

Millicent inserted her pinky into one of the spaces where a tooth used to be. "Guatemala is full of expats. Most come for the cheap lifestyle."

She frowned when she said this, as if she didn't consider that a valid reason. "I stayed because I wanted to help."

She pulled her black sweater around herself more tightly. Her office was so small and dark, I felt as if I were in a confessional.

"Years ago," Millicent said. "I donated a lot of money to an order of nuns in Zaragoza. They built a food center for kids. It was more like an orphanage, though, because the kids were starving and their families couldn't feed them. They had a party when it opened and invited the donors. A priest gave the blessing and led the tour."

Millicent's wrinkled cheeks lifted in a faint smile, proud of the church's activist history in Guatemala.

"The kids slept in a nursery behind the center," Millicent said. She slid the shoebox full of passports behind the framed photo of

Toño to show me the center's configuration. "They had blankets and toy boxes. Cribs and beds. Mobiles hanging from the ceiling. Anything you could want."

As she stared down at the shoebox and framed photo, her eyes became glassy. She seemed to forget I was sitting across the desk from her. "During the tour, behind one of the cribs, I noticed wires in a snarl, like a rat's nest. But everybody was so happy, I didn't comment on it. I didn't want to spoil the mood."

She pulled a handkerchief out of her top drawer and pressed it to her nose.

"One night there was a short circuit. Sparks flew, onto a blanket they think. Two teenage girls from the neighborhood heard the screaming, but it was too late. Every baby was lost."

She buried her face in the handkerchief. "If only I'd said something."

I tried to offer some feeble comfort. "They're angels in heaven."

"I have to believe that," Millicent said. "I can't live with myself otherwise."

Neither one of us moved for what felt like forever. Danger lurked everywhere.

Chapter 14

DAY OF THE DEAD

My obsession with finishing the adoption was matched only by my obsession to get Olivia to consider me her mother. And, frankly, finishing the adoption felt like the easier task. Because at least with the adoption, I could write daily goals on my to-do list and cross them off. "Meet with Rodríguez, check status of other mothers' cases, follow-up with Gilda. Pick up renewed passport from Millicent."

Whereas I couldn't *make* Olivia love me. I could hold her and feed her, teach her to walk and to talk. I could point to myself and say "Mommy" until she mimicked the word. But that didn't mean she loved me or trusted me or felt safer with me than with anyone else.

The more time I spent with her, the more I understood that her strongest emotion seemed to be confusion. In a year and a half, she had had four different mothers: Ana, Griselda Chávez in Febrero Fourth, Lupe, and myself. Each one seemed like she would be *Mamá* forever. And then, just like that, each of them was gone. It was no mystery why Olivia turned her face when I tried to kiss her, or sucked on her own sleeve for comfort if she stumbled and fell. Three mothers had abandoned her already.

Because Kendra had taken custody of Susanna as a baby, she didn't face the same challenge. Nor did Mary Kay or Heather. Of course, they might not have admitted feeling rejected even if they did. Feeling rejected by your own child was not something most mothers cared to broadcast.

"Attachment" was understood intuitively by adoptive parents, but when I asked my mother and sisters about it, they didn't understand the question. "Attachment" was not a concept they had heard of, much less dealt with. They were sure that once we got home and Olivia settled into a routine, we would become closer. I didn't have the heart to tell them that the issue seemed deeper than that. That something between us was not right.

I fretted about it constantly. As I watched Olivia methodically stack plastic containers on her high chair tray, or line up her stuffed animals in a row on the sofa, I wondered whether her compulsion to order objects was normal, or a symptom of her need to control her external environment. If I tried to get her to make eye contact and she avoided my gaze, I questioned whether she was simply busy doing something else or incapable of connecting. I forced her to look at me by putting my face in her line of vision and debated whether her gaze was sincere. I was no psychologist, but it felt as though a part of Olivia remained in reserve. She was afraid to let down her guard.

When Tim called, I unloaded on him my litany of worries. Would Olivia be able to form close friendships as a child and intimate relationships as an adult? Or was she doomed to a life of solitude, unable to connect with others? Had I inflicted irreparable damage on her by not moving to Guatemala sooner? Was I one more unreliable mother figure she was reluctant to trust?

"Maybe the problems started with the baby jogger," I said. "I should have carried her everywhere, the way Kendra carries Susanna."

"Stop right there," Tim said. "Olivia is a year older than Susanna and ten pounds heavier. Carrying her across town or to the grocery store isn't feasible."

"Guatemalan women strap their babies in slings across their backs and carry them until the children are four."

"Guatemalan women balance baskets on their heads and give birth in the fields."

He reassured me that although I felt inadequate, my constant presence would eventually convince Olivia that I was the person who would never leave her.

More than anything, I wanted this to be true.

Not helping matters were the weekly phone calls from Lupe, which always ended with her begging to see Olivia.

Except Lupe called her Stefany. I didn't correct her. Olivia's new name represented our new life together, and our new life together was something I didn't want to share. I wasn't proud of that fact, but it was undeniable. For a year, Lupe had had Olivia to herself. Now it was my turn.

Lupe said she couldn't sleep without Stefany. She couldn't eat. Francisco had bought her a puppy—a puppy!—and I heard the scorn in her voice, the impossibility of any dog ever replacing Stefany.

"I'm sorry," I offered, aware of how unconvincing that response must have felt to her.

But I didn't give in. In my elementary Spanish, I tried to communicate the word *confusing*. As in, *la niña* calls me *Mamá*, I think *la niña* is beginning to love me. My intention was not to hurt Lupe. My intention was to create stability and continuity for my child. I couldn't allow Lupe to reappear in Olivia's life only to disappear again.

I had spent four months working toward this. Please don't ask me to erase it.

Lupe was still begging when I hung up.

On November 1, everyone in Guatemala flocked to their local cemetery to fly kites. November 1 was Day of the Dead, and kites were believed to be a conduit through which the living could communicate with the spirits of the deceased.

For weeks the country had been preparing, with kites under construction everywhere: in restaurants hanging from rafters, in the central courtyard of the language school, at the *mercado*. Made from cut-up paper and pasted onto bamboo frames, they were as colorful as crazy quilts. Most ranged from six inches to ten feet across, although the *barriletes gigantes* topped twenty or thirty feet.

Many villages capitalized on the kites' popularity by hosting competitions to judge the biggest and best. Thousands of people showed up to view the contests. One of the most famous took place in a cemetery in Santiago, Sacatepéquez, ten miles outside Antigua.

Saturday morning, five minutes after I hung up from Lupe's most recent phone call, Kendra stopped by to invite Olivia and me to go to Santiago. She had reserved seats for her and Susanna on a shuttle bus and was sure they had extra room.

"You've never seen anything like it," she said. "Four guys run alongside one kite to get it aloft."

I considered going—the kites really were spectacular—but ultimately declined. The prospect of being dropped off at a cemetery ten miles away, among thousands of strangers who may or may not have reacted favorably to my being with Olivia, scared me. "Not that you shouldn't go," I hastily added.

We agreed that I should at least visit the small cemetery in Antigua, San Lázaro, which was tucked in behind the *mercado*, beyond the bus terminal. While Kendra couldn't guarantee San Lázaro would feature kites, at least it would give me an idea of how the holiday was celebrated. Kendra promised to take pictures in Santiago.

I headed to San Lázaro with Olivia after breakfast. The day was clear and warm, just a bit windy—ideal for flying kites. Mindful of my discussion with Tim and believing it would be better for Olivia, I carried her instead of rolling her in the jogger. She seemed thrilled by her elevated perch, and I liked the feeling of her hugging my neck. As a bonus, my arms would get a workout. The walk to and from San Lázaro was about three miles, and by my estimate, she was three feet tall and weighed about twenty-five pounds. I sang "The Alphabet Song" along the way.

We crossed the Square diagonally, passing the fountain in the center, the ice cream vendors and shoeshiners, the groups of Americans on park benches thumbing through guide books. We bypassed the Arch over Fifth Avenida, and turned up the street toward the grocery store and on to Alameda Santa Lucía and the *mercado*.

The cemetery was behind a wrought-iron fence at the end of a dead-end street. In front of the fence, vendors did a brisk business selling grave blankets of pine needles and yellow marigolds—traditional in Guatemala—along with snacks of salted corn-on-the-cob and filled *pupusas*. A mime in white-face entertained an audience with a trapped-in-an-imaginary-box routine, while two girls paraded by on stilts.

Behind the gate, San Lázaro looked like a cemetery in New Orleans: hundreds of white-stone mausoleums and family-size crypts, topped with crosses of every variety and size. Dozens of family groups were meandering through them, pausing in front of this or that monument to pay their respects. In the middle of the cemetery was a small church, also white. The steps were strewn with pine needles and marigolds, with a string quartet seated among them.

I walked toward one row of mausoleums to get a better look at the family names, searching for Olivia's. Then I realized San Lázaro was a final resting place for the well-to-do. It was extremely unlikely that an indigenous family from Toto would have ended up there.

Likewise, few indigenous families were gathered to pay their respects. I didn't see any kites, either. In fact, as I moved down the cobblestone lane among the mausoleums, I realized that the biggest attraction seemed to be Olivia and me. Everyone was staring and pointing at us, as though trying to figure out who we were and what our relationship was.

"Haven't they seen a mother and daughter before?" I asked Olivia. Without other American parents around, I felt uncomfortable and conspicuous. Kendra had the right idea, going to Santiago. We were more anonymous in a bigger crowd. It was easier to blend in. I had planned to stay at San Lázaro for the afternoon, but it felt as if it were time to go.

Olivia, however, had no intention of leaving. She was perfectly content at the cemetery. She scrambled from my arms to inspect the pine needles, then swept the cobblestones as though with a tiny broom. She discovered that a mausoleum substituted nicely for a play structure, so much more interesting than the usual cathedral steps. And the sounds made by the string quartet were definitely worth investigating. Olivia took my hand and steered me toward the players for closer inspection.

As I followed her to the church steps, I hoped that the families who had been whispering about us were watching. *See?* I wanted to say. *We don't look alike, but I am her mother. It's been a long road to get here, but I am her mother.*

No need to reveal to those families the depths of my real doubts. My fear that some part of Olivia would never—could never—belong to me, in the effortless way their children belonged to them. Such defeatist thoughts would get me nowhere. It was like riding a bicycle up a very steep hill: Never think about getting to the top; deal only with what was two feet ahead.

I concentrated on listening to the music with Olivia. In the mournful strains of the violins, I recognized Pachelbel's "Canon" and the recognition cheered me. *Revel in this moment as it's happening,* I told myself. The quartet finished the Canon and waited while the assembled audience applauded. I hitched Olivia up to my hip and she looped her arm around my shoulder. Tim had been right. She was finally beginning to trust me. Baby steps.

I carried Olivia into the church and slipped into a back pew. Churches in Guatemala were simple—whitewashed walls and wooden rafters, stone floor, candles to be lit by the faithful—and this one was no exception. After uttering a silent prayer asking for strength, I lifted Olivia higher in my arms so her head rested against my shoulder. The morning's activities had worn her out.

She slept right through the sounds of the string quartet as I carried her down the stairs, and she didn't stir as I swished through the pine needles and marigolds, back to the street among the stilt-walkers and mimes. Through the *mercado*, across Santa Lucía, and toward the Square. If I was lucky, she would stay asleep for a good nap, allowing me to get a rest, too. Carrying her definitely added to my workout.

Almost home. I rounded the fountain in the middle of the Square and continued across the diagonal when Lupe stood up from a park bench and blocked my path.

"Lupe? What are you doing here?"

"*La luz de mi vida*," Lupe cried. "The light of my life."

She reached for Olivia and grabbed her from me. Olivia's cheek was crusty from sleep and stuck to my shoulder. Olivia roused from her nap and sat straight. "*Mamá*," she said to me, and registering that it was Lupe, said to her, "*Mamá?*"

Sweat gushed from my every pore. I felt as if I were on fire. My impulse was to tackle Lupe and grab Olivia. Run with her, to any-place as long as it was far.

Lupe glowered at me. "You promised I could visit."

"But that was before I understood what's best for Olivia. Not best for you or me. Best for Olivia. Only one *mamá*. That's what she needs."

Or was it?

As I stood in the Square, my hands clenched at my sides, doubt insinuated itself into my brain. How could I be so sure what was best for Olivia? What if I was making things worse?

Lupe pulled Olivia close, kissed her on the cheek. But Olivia's body was rigid. Her eyes were round and terrified. Now Lupe was the stranger.

If I grabbed Olivia, might bystanders think I was kidnapping her?

I kept my voice calm. "How did you know I would be here?"

"*Día de los Muertos*," she answered. "Day of the Dead."

She had known that at some time during the day I would walk through the Square. Everyone did. She admitted she had been on the bench since noon.

Lupe pointed with her head to the Garzas' maroon Camry, creeping toward Fourth Avenida Sur. Francisco was at the wheel. He had been waiting, too. He would meet us at my house.

"Meet us for what?"

Lupe didn't answer. She had redistributed Olivia's weight and was carrying her lengthwise across her forearms. Olivia looked like a corpse. I grabbed one ankle and walked beside Lupe holding onto it. We walked the five blocks in silence.

I unlocked the front door to our *casita* and stepped in first. Lupe followed me with Olivia, turning sideways to fit through the door. Francisco stepped in next. Not wanting them to come in, I didn't move from the front hallway. Neither did they. Olivia was a blank. I was still holding her ankle.

"She's tired," I said. "She needs to sleep."

As casually as I could manage, I slipped my hands under her

hips and shifted her from Lupe's arms into mine. Her body collapsed as though she were boneless. "I will take her upstairs."

Lupe thrust out both hands to stop me. "*Maribel está embarazada.*" "My sixteen-year-old daughter is pregnant."

Maribel in her Dr. Martens and heavy eyeliner.

Lupe rounded her hands over her belly to show me how big. "Four months."

About the time Olivia had left the family. Lupe had been so disconsolate, maybe Maribel wanted to create a substitute child.

"You will be a grandmother," I said. "Congratulations."

Lupe cupped her hands to her cheeks to demonstrate her despair. The father was a boy from Pollo Campero, where Maribel had worked since dropping out of school. He had no plans to marry her. For a strange, uncomfortable moment, I wondered if Lupe expected me to offer to adopt her grandchild. Lupe clarified. Maribel would stay at home with Lupe and Francisco. They would raise the baby as their own.

"*Por supuesto,*" I agreed. "Of course you will."

I moved to take Olivia upstairs.

"*Necesitamos mucho,*" Lupe said. "We need a lot. Can you help us?"

"Anything you want." I gestured to the living room with one arm. "*Todo.*" "All of it."

Lupe didn't ask twice. She made a beeline toward Olivia's old stroller, useless on Antigua's cobblestone streets, stored in a corner of the entry hall. After handing it to Francisco, she headed for the armoire in the living room and scooped up two packages of disposable diapers, a three-pack of bottles, and two cans of baby formula. When I moved past her to carry Olivia upstairs, Lupe didn't even pause. She would take anything that wasn't nailed down, I was sure of it. Thankfully, Olivia was fast asleep and didn't have to witness the dismantling.

When I returned, Francisco was outside loading the car, and Lupe was in my kitchen filling plastic grocery bags with pasta, rice, coffee, and cheese. She had even managed to ferret out my stash of Nestlé Crunch bars, my late-night solace when I sat alone at the dining room table studying my Spanish and missing Tim.

I helped Lupe carry the final load out to the car and hugged her and Francisco. There were no tears when we said goodbye.

I stood by my front door and waved as the Camry bumped down Fourth Avenida and toward the volcano. Three hours of daylight remained. When Olivia woke from her nap, I'd take her to Hotel Antigua for a swim.

My heart felt much lighter than it had that morning. The specter of Lupe had been hanging over me for more than a year, making me doubt whether Olivia would ever accept me as her mother. Now I knew she would. Nobody, not even Lupe, could change that.

Lupe never came to Antigua again.

Chapter 15

ENTREPRENEURS

It felt as though everyone in Antigua was selling something. They knocked on our front door peddling magnifying glasses, liter bottles of soda, smelly fish in a box on the back of a bicycle. On the sidewalk, girls advertised handicrafts and women offered tortillas. A wizened old lady charged one *quetzal* to step on her bathroom scale. A blind man with no legs hawked songs from his radio. Shining shoes was big business: Old-timers claimed established spots outside the *mercado* and on the Square; boys canvassed the streets toting their wooden kits, ready to drop to one knee at a moment's notice.

One of the most lucrative enterprises was washing cars. I learned this from Mary Kay, the only one of the mothers to rent one. She was from suburban Dallas and claimed she couldn't function without one. She had an energetic boy and his gear to haul around and figured, "What's another fifty bucks a day when you're spending thousands?"

Mary Kay and I stood together on the curb outside Conexión

and watched two school-age boys rinse soap from her car with what seemed like less water than I used to brush my teeth.

"They're each in charge of a block," Mary Kay said. "If you park on their block, you pay them five *quetzales* and they *watch* your car to make sure nobody steals it. As a bonus, they *wash* it with their bucket of dirty water."

The boys wiped down the car with some shredded rags.

"The first time I parked, I slammed the door and walked away. I didn't know the drill. When I came back, I couldn't find my car. I didn't recognize it. They'd stripped off every scrap of chrome. Hubcaps, antenna, the letters that spelled 'Ford.' Now I tell them"—she pointed to her right eye with her index finger— "*Watch* the car. Not *wash*."

"Do they get that?"

"They get that I give them five *quetzales*. That they get."

Mary Kay lifted one shoulder, world-weary and resigned. "Everybody in this country has got their hand out, which you will learn soon enough if you haven't by now."

She opened her change purse and selected some coins. "People are poor here. Their hands are out for a reason."

After leaving Mary Kay, Olivia and I did what we often did after checking email and before going to the pool. We went to the *mercado* to shop. I really didn't need another tablecloth or woven shawl, but the objects were so appealing and the level of craftsmanship so high, I couldn't resist the temptation. I missed looking at art, an activity I had taken for granted during the years I worked in an art museum. Walking among the stalls was as close as I could get to replicating the experience.

Paintings were my special weakness. I was a sucker for an unusual perspective: the Square seen from the second floor of the *Municipalidad*, Volcano Agua from an interior courtyard, or anything that was a *vista de pájaro* (bird's-eye view). Oil paintings with a matte finish especially appealed to me. I loved religious themes, paintings on board or sheets of aluminum, or works with an edgy, political message. I learned which artists were from Lake Atitlán, which were from the capital, and who lived in Antigua. Before long, I was able to recognize the work of individual artists before I read their signature.

My favorite was a painting that would never be sold in the *mercado*, the one I had discovered my first day in Antigua: *Feliz Viaje* by Óscar Perén, commonly known as *The Guatemalan Bus*. There was something about the crazy anarchy of the colorful scene—the squawking chickens; the crowded seats; the scowling, smoking bus driver underneath the sign that said *"No Fumar"*— that made me smile every time I looked at it. One of the sellers displayed a book on the art of Guatemala, *Arte Naïf*, and I learned that not only was Perén one of the country's most respected living painters, he lived less than an hour away from Antigua in the mountain village of Comalapa.

My cab driver, Juan Carlos, had never heard of Óscar Perén, or any of the other painters based in Comalapa, but he was game for finding Perén's studio.

I almost expected Óscar Perén's Comalapa to be like other artists' outposts I'd visited. A row of studios with glass front windows. Inside, spare, industrial spaces and gallery attendants dressed in black.

But Comalapa was nothing like that. It was a farming community, with a central town surrounded by cornfields and beanfields. The streets were narrow and dusty, with no tourist directory to indicate where the artists lived. To someone like me, who had spent years working in the museum world, the lack of commercialism was as unbelievable as it was refreshing. Yet art pervaded the village. Murals covered stone walls. Houses were painted with stripes the color of azure and terra cotta. The *huipils* on the local women were a brilliant light blue, embroidered with red and orange.

In the middle of town, I spied a sign posted with an arrow. Óscar Perén.

Juan Carlos turned at the church and we headed uphill. A large fresco on the exterior wall of a house indicated we'd found the right place.

Perén's ten-year-old grandson, Hectór, greeted me at the front door. The boy was courtly and formal, and spoke English perfectly. "My grandfather is working in his studio next door. I shall call him."

Perén's gallery shimmered with color. From ceiling to floor, every inch of wall space was covered with his paintings. Pictures of market scenes, religious ceremonies, and children at play. Buses, cathedral ruins, and hot air balloons. The gallery had only one small window, but the space felt filled with light.

As a young man, Óscar Perén had been a farmer, and as he entered the room, I saw he retained the stocky build of a man who had tilled the soil. His searing brown eyes missed nothing: my white skin and blonde hair; Juan Carlos, visible through the small window, sitting in the front seat of his taxi. Perén smelled like acrylic paint.

His presence was serious and reserved. As I gushed about my favorite details of *The Guatemalan Bus*, he rubbed his chin, glancing occasionally at Hectór for clarification. When I finished, Perén excused himself and left the gallery. Suddenly, I felt so American: barging into an artist's studio unannounced, raving about a picture that had previously received international acclaim. Would I have dared do the same to a famous American artist?

Unsure if I should apologize, I defaulted to my usual art-viewing behavior: clasped my hands behind my back and gazed appraisingly at the other canvases. Hectór hovered beside me with a feather duster, grazing it along the tops of each frame. Whenever he sensed me pause in front of a picture, he delivered a practiced speech: "This painting depicts Comalapa before the earthquake. Notice the houses that are no longer standing. Here we have a scene from Kite-Flying Day. See the different designs?"

Óscar Perén returned with a stretched canvas. It was *The Guatemalan Bus*, the paint not completely dry. He removed the Kite-Flying painting from the wall and carefully replaced it with *Feliz Viaje*. Cocking his head, he adjusted it a millimeter, stepped back, tweaked it again.

As delighted as I was to see the picture, I was more surprised. I had assumed the original hung in a museum.

Hectór explained. "Many people want this picture. My grandfather paints many copies."

Óscar Perén may have been Guatemala's most famous living artist, but he did what he must in order to survive. He sold me the painting, and because it wasn't yet dry, personally delivered it to my *casita* the next Sunday afternoon. Whenever I look at it in my living room in California, I remember Óscar Perén standing at the front door, my copy of *Feliz Viaje* rolled up under his arm.

One of the canniest, most aggressive vendors in Antigua—and maybe all of Guatemala—was a woman named Rose. Her territory was right in the middle of the Square near the fountain, and there she sat on the ground every day with her twelve-year-old daughter, dressed in the *traje* of the village of nearby Aguas Calientes.

"Table cloths, napkins, case for makeup. Good price," they called out to passing tourists. Or at least Rose called out. Her twelve-year-old-daughter, Dorothy, hunched beside her mother, as silent as a figure in a wax museum.

Kendra and I swore that Rose sized up potential buyers based on the condition of their sandals and brand of digital camera. In another setting, with different opportunities, she might have been a litigation attorney or corporate raider. But here in Antigua, she was a super-seller of *típica*. Twice I bought wall hangings from her that I didn't much like, but Rose's persistence wore me down.

Kendra decided that she would like to buy some purses from Rose, wholesale, and sell them for a profit back home. When she was in the Peace Corps she had toyed with the idea, and had since regretted she didn't try it then. Now she was in a better financial position to make an investment.

"She might figure out a way to export them herself," I told Kendra.

"I have to find the right approach," Kendra said.

For a few mornings, we observed Rose in action. First, we saw that she drove a very nice car which she parked on a side street under the watchful eye of a car-washer. Then, we saw that the car's trunk was loaded with *típica*, piles of which Rose dropped off to other vendors. Finally, we saw that she didn't dress in *traje* at all, but affected it as a costume. She changed from her black stretch pants in the ladies' room at Pollo Campero.

"She's a sly one," Kendra said.

Kendra forged a friendship with Rose, stopping by every morning on her way to Conexión, and checking in during the afternoon before dinner. After about a week, Rose invited Kendra to her home in Aguas Calientes to negotiate.

The next morning at Conexión, I couldn't wait for her report.

"Well?" I said as I met her outside.

It turned out that Rose was willing to give Kendra a good price on purses, but only on one condition. Kendra must take Dorothy, Rose's daughter, as part of the deal.

"Rose says Dorothy isn't any good at selling," Kendra said. "And Rose has six other mouths to feed."

"What does she expect you to do?"

"Adopt her." Kendra sighed. "Rose said 'What will her life be like if she stays here?'"

Neither Kendra nor I knew what Dorothy's life would be like, to be honest, but at least she would be in the only home she had known for twelve years. Putting food on the table didn't seem to be an issue for Rose. Dorothy as dead weight seemed more like it. We worried about accusations of payments to birth mothers. This sounded worse. This was a businesswoman offering a discount on purses, with her daughter as an incentive.

For a lot of people, adoption was a business just like anything else. As long as we were taking one child, we might as well take another.

November 8: day one hundred in Antigua. Gilda came through. Sixteen months after we filed our Power of Attorney, we were in PGN. Gilda picked up the file from Family Court. Rodríguez called me himself to tell me Gilda delivered the file in the morning.

"You will process it quickly?" I asked.

"*Rápido,*" he said.

"One week?"

"*Vamos a ver,*" he said. "We'll see."

I usually didn't call Tim during the day, but I did to share the latest development.

"We can't rest on our laurels," Tim said. "We've got to stay on him. Go twice a week. Every day."

"He's got other things to do besides meet with me," I said. "Besides, I don't want to be too obvious. People at PGN might think something's going on."

"That Guatemalan friend of your sister's—Teresa. She brought wine and chocolate. Bake him cookies. Give him a baseball cap. We need to be proactive."

"You mean *I* need to be proactive. I'm the one doing everything."

"Somebody's got to make the money to pay the bills," Tim said. "Speaking of which, I have to go. Don't let me down, Jess. I'm counting on you."

To keep our angst in check, Kendra and I met at the gym two afternoons a week. My pattern was to feed Olivia lunch and walk her twice around the block in the jogger so she fell asleep for a short nap before the fun began with Aracely and Junior.

Like the Fuente Café, the gym had been converted to its current use from its original incarnation as private residence. A *pila* shaped like a lotus blossom stood in for the fountain. The gym was open-air, with no roof. On days when it rained, the ground in the courtyard turned to wet, muddy muck, so that part of every workout included jumping over puddles to dash to the next machine.

The gym charged about $3 per visit, which at first seemed like a bargain. But after a few months in Antigua, I regarded money in terms of the local economy and $3 no longer seemed cheap. I was thinking in *quetzales*, not dollars, in the same way I sometimes thought in Spanish and not English. When the gym advertised a discount for students, I marched to the front desk to qualify, explaining that I was a language student. The front desk referred the question to the owner, a muscular, toned *Ladina* whom I'd seen driving around town in a red convertible. She ruled that language students didn't qualify. When I later recounted the tale to my Spanish teacher, Lila, she observed that the only people who could afford the gym were rich *Antigüeños* and Americans. They shouldn't have expected a discount because they didn't need one. I couldn't argue with her logic.

I rode the stationary bike and tried to read whatever copy of the latest Spanish newspaper was lying around. Kendra rowed on the gym's one creaky rowing machine while Susanna smiled at passersby from a blanket beside her. Susanna was young enough that she stayed put wherever Kendra set her down.

Peddling hard on the stationary bike, I exerted myself enough to get my heart rate up, but Kendra pulled on her oars like the Iron-man competitor she was. Drenched in sweat, she pumped and glided with the steady, powerful rhythm of a turbine at Hoover Dam. She created a stir among the other gym-goers: Antigua women with velour track suits and hair that never mussed. Their treadmills slowed to a stop and fell silent as they literally forgot to put one foot in front of another, so distracted were they by Kendra's athletic prowess.

Afterward, Kendra changed into a dry T-shirt while I arranged mats on the floor for our sit-ups, push-ups, and stretches. I was in fairly good shape myself, but no matter how many repetitions of anything I could do, Kendra could do exponentially more. After I got to know her better, I realized she didn't intend to show off. She was just strong. With Tim so far away, I was happy to have Kendra to lean on. Our post-workout talks were as therapeutic for me as the workout itself.

During a Tuesday workout, Kendra paused during her sit-ups to fill me in on a trip she had taken to her former Peace Corps village the previous weekend. In some ways, nothing had changed in the village, but in others, everything had. Children had grown up to be parents; mothers were grandmothers. Almost an entire generation had moved to the U.S. to find work: eight children from one family gone, six children from another.

The village elders remembered and embraced Kendra, but Susanna had left them puzzled. Why would someone from the United States want a baby from Guatemala?

"They kept asking why her mother gave her away," Kendra said. "Three villages over, someone gave away her baby. When her neighbors found out, they cut off her hair with a machete."

She hugged her knees to her chest. "They love babies here. Babies, babies, babies. But how do they take care of them when they're older? They send them to work when they're nine."

She looked at me plaintively, as though I might have had an answer. I threw up my hands.

Kendra's main frustration was that she still didn't have DNA. In an effort to be supportive, I reminded her of the advice she once gave me: commit one action every week to advance her case. This, I told her, was what I did to feel empowered. "Even if you aren't accomplishing anything," I said, "you'll feel like you are."

Kendra laughed. We both believed in thinking positive.

Kendra took my advice and the next week pushed her agency to get Febi's DNA test. Because Febi couldn't read or write, she signed the form with a thumbprint. Febi's older sister acted as Febi's guardian.

I had never met anyone who witnessed a DNA test; the fact that Kendra somehow finagled her way in confirmed for me her insider status. During our workout that week, I sat close to her on a mat as she recounted the details.

"It was downstairs in an office building in Guatemala City,"

Kendra said. "The foster mothers were there with their babies. Then someone brought in the birth mothers."

I stared at her raptly. "I'd be afraid to meet Olivia's birth mother. Weren't you nervous?"

"Susanna didn't recognize her," Kendra said.

"What did Febi do?"

"Pretended she didn't care. Acted cool." Kendra lifted her chin defiantly to demonstrate.

"Tragic," I said.

"They scraped the inside of Susanna's mouth first. Really hard, like they were scraping away the whole inside. I've never heard her scream like that."

We looked at Susanna, asleep on her blanket, her arms and legs sprawled open defenselessly.

My tongue rubbed the inside of my own cheek. "Did you find out any new information?"

"The orphanage director had told me the birth father was Febi's boss, an older man with another family who had Febi on the side. But when I said that, Febi got very insulted. '*No! Fue un chico. Mi novio.*'" "A young guy. My boyfriend."

"The older man must be a standard story. Other mothers say the same thing."

Kendra folded a corner of Susanna's blanket over the baby's legs. "At least I can tell Susanna she was conceived in love."

"Anything else about Febi?"

"Her favorite food is Pollo Campero."

"Join the club."

"Febi's very pretty and shy," Kendra said. "I could be her grand-mother."

Kendra was told Susanna's adoption might be problematic, but she had had no inkling what that would mean. Now that Febi's mother was dead, and her sister was Febi's guardian, the sister must be appointed guardian to all ten brothers and sisters.

Kendra stretched her legs out in front of her. "But because each of the siblings has a different father, the attorney has to place public notices in the newspaper to find every one of them to get their permission."

She turned to me as if to gauge my reaction. I lay back on the floor and bent my knees, pretending I was about to do crunches. Ten different fathers? Notices in the newspaper? To begin with, how many people in Guatemala knew how to read, much less read the daily newspaper. Kendra's situation sounded untenable, but I couldn't tell her that.

Kendra looked over her shoulder to make sure no one was listening. "The orphanage director said she had to spend $2,000 of her own money. Then she tells me Susanna isn't worth it."

I sat straight up, indignant. "That's something Yolanda would say."

"I hate this place," Kendra said. "Everyone thinks I love it, but I don't. I hate it."

She pulled her knees in and wrapped her arms around them. "When I was in the Peace Corps, I knew an American married to an indigenous woman. Two gorgeous children. They ran an eco-resort in the jungle. The military said he needed to pay for their protection, but he refused. What does he need protection from? So they chopped off his head. Stuck it on a pole for everyone to see."

She pressed both her palms against her eye sockets, as if to blot out the scene playing inside her eyelids. "When I left, I vowed never to come back." Her voice was muffled. "I should have kept my promise."

I reached over and placed one hand on the middle of Kendra's back.

"You came back for Susanna," I said. "We'll get through this."

She kept pressing on her eyes, as if I hadn't said anything.

Chapter 16

THE FIX

Day 110: almost four months in Antigua. With Thanksgiving around the corner, the stakes felt even higher because on the heels of Thanksgiving was Christmas, when PGN closed for two weeks. The huge backlog of cases would grow even huger. Nobody would get out until well after New Year's.

I felt trapped. It was the randomness that was so crazy-making—the lack of reason to any of it. Based on *what* did a case get to the top of the pile? No one could explain it to me, not even Señor Rodríguez. Suddenly he too was claiming *mañana*. I needed a Plan B. Something else to try.

Back home, supplies were being laid in for cranberry sauce, giblet gravy, my mother's famous two-tone cheesecake. The big day would be ushered in by the Radio City Music Hall Rockettes, high-kicking in the Macy's Day Parade. My mother would be in her usual frenzy, directing my sisters and the girls in the kitchen—*Potatoes need to be peeled!*

Yams sliced! We forgot to get baking powder for the biscuits!—while my father and the boys watched football. At three o'clock, the family would sit down for dinner. Bowing their heads, they'd say grace.

My old life was so easy. How could I have known how easy it was?

I went to church with Olivia and we lit candles in every color. Blue for legal matters, yellow for faith, green for lost causes. I knelt with her in front of the tomb of Hermano Pedro, Guatemala's first and only saint. My prayer remained constant: *Please, please, please. Get us out of PGN.*

"I want you to listen carefully to what I'm going to tell you."

Mary Kay's voice sounded urgent over my cell phone. We had just left her and her son Joaquín at the Hotel Antigua pool an hour earlier. She'd seemed fine then. "But you have to promise not to tell anyone else."

I turned off the water I was boiling for elbow noodles. Olivia stood on a chair beside me stacking her plastic containers on the kitchen counter. Mary Kay never called during dinner hour. My heart began to pound. "I promise."

"Cheryl has a contact in PGN. Pay $600 and you're done."

I reached for the counter to steady myself. For months I'd suspected people were paying bribes. What I couldn't figure out was how much and to whom. I'd wondered whether it was Señor Rodríguez himself. What a fool I'd been, going to PGN every Monday to meet with him, proving to anyone who might have been noticing that I was a devoted, caring mother. Now it turned out the waiting could end for $600. Could it be that easy?

"Is anyone else doing it?"

"Cheryl offered it to me. And to Catherine and Ruby."

Catherine and Ruby who lived in the condo complex on the north side of town, who seemed so confident they would get out, who rarely came to the pool. That explained why they stayed apart.

Mary Kay continued: "Cheryl said she could only do one more person. I said your baby's the oldest. You have to act fast."

A wave of panic rushed through me. All of us mothers were on a sinking ship and there weren't enough life vests to go around. I glanced down at Olivia, who was no longer playing with her plastic containers, but staring at me as though she understood the gravity of the conversation.

"Call Cheryl tonight," Mary Kay said. "Don't blow this."

I opened the sliding glass door to the courtyard to get better phone reception to the U.S. The air was cool. What if this was a trick so they could see who was giving bribes? What if they took those families' babies away? The Embassy could be in on it. So could UNICEF. This could be their strategy to finally shut down adoptions forever.

I peered through the sliding glass door into the dining room. Olivia cowered under the table, gnawing on her knuckle.

I had been in PGN on Monday for my weekly visit. My mind flashed on the faces of the office workers bent over their desks. Every face was as unreadable as a poker player's. Even when I bumped into an assistant who appeared friendly in the ladies' room or hallway and begged, "Please, can't you help me?" they gave me nothing, not one iota of hope. They turned and walked away as if they hadn't heard me.

Maybe this explained why PGN kicked out cases for ridiculous reasons—an expired notary stamp, a request for a new copy of a birth certificate, another "good manners" letter attesting to the adoptive parents' moral character. Not to mention the entire Hague debacle.

I sat on the concrete edge of the *pila* and hunched my shoulders away from Olivia. We'd wasted so much time already, and for what? For a lousy six hundred bucks. Olivia was eighteen months old.

My index finger shook as I pressed the key for speed dial. Tim. He'd know what to do. He could decide whether or not we should trust Cheryl. I cupped my hand around the mouthpiece. Did technology exist to eavesdrop on cell phones? And if so, did they have access to it in Guatemala?

Pick up the phone, I wanted to scream. *It's five o'clock in California. Where are you?*

Tim sounded as if I were interrupting him.

"We've been offered a deal," I said. I told him the price.

"I knew there had to be a way."

I laid out the details. For eight years, Cheryl had run one of the

biggest agencies that adopted from Guatemala. She was socially connected to important people in the capital.

"When I met her at the pool, she was sitting with the wife of a Guatemalan attorney. This is Mary Kay's second adoption. She's been through
it already. She wouldn't do it if she didn't think it was necessary."

"We don't have a choice," Tim said.

I didn't expect him to agree so easily. "What if it's a trap?"

"Call Cheryl. We're in."

Cheryl wanted the money in crisp, clean twenty-dollar bills. No tears
or nicks. No ink marks. Her contact worked inside PGN. Cheryl
never called him or her by name; she always said "the contact," in
her smoker's voice. The contact needed Olivia's birth name and birth
date. Our names, our case number, her birth mother's name.

"Paying money makes me nervous," I whispered into my cell
phone. I couldn't say the word "bribe."

Cheryl cleared her throat. "It's how they do business."

"What if someone finds out?" I was trembling so hard my teeth
were chattering.

Cheryl coughed.

"Impossible." She made a hacking sound. "I'll meet you at ten
thirty tomorrow morning at Café Vienna. Nobody hears this."

I ran upstairs with Olivia. I set her on the bedroom floor
and pulled open the night table drawer where I kept my money

in a zippered bag. I dumped the contents of the bag onto the bed-spread. Three of the twenties were wrinkled and torn. The rest I'd converted to *quetzales*. I counted $400 only. Stepping onto the rooftop terrace, I dialed Tim again.

"You either have to express mail me the money or get on a plane," I said.

"I'm supposed to mule money to Guatemala?"

"Muling money is the easy part. I'm the one who has to meet with Cheryl."

"I'll be there in a week for Thanksgiving," Tim said. "I'll bring it then. Cheryl said she doesn't need the money until the end."

I stifled the rage that welled up inside me, despising Tim for his rationality. He wanted me to do the dirty work. "Fine. I'll see you in a week."

I hung up without saying goodbye.

The next morning, everything was the same, but different. Instead of pausing to chat as usual, Paola rushed directly upstairs to make the bed as though I were radiating a bad smell. The two kids who washed parked cars on our block crossed the street as soon as I opened the front door. The commuters at the bus stop on the corner seemed to sneer.

I strapped Olivia into the baby jogger and pushed her across the Square. No way I'd risk someone grabbing her from my arms.

I would have sworn that the tortilla vendors and the *típica* sellers, the taxi drivers and the bank guards—people I'd smiled at every day since August—watched me with a mixture of contempt and pity. Contempt because of what I was about to do. Pity because it might work; and pity because it might not. They understood full well how corrupt the adoption process was. As corrupt as every other bureaucracy they interacted with every day of their lives.

Theodore had said the workers inside PGN were laughing at me. And our *notario*, Simón Guerrero, had locked Tim and me into his office with an ominous warning: "Things are different here." Guerrero was right: We weren't close to being in control. He had urged us not to get in over our heads. I was drowning.

I picked my way across the cobblestones as though the information Cheryl requested that I carried in my backpack was a live hand grenade. I was singularly ill-equipped to be involved in this brand of subterfuge. I had never watched a *James Bond* movie or a single episode of *Law & Order*, in any of its incarnations. I couldn't read Scott Turow or even Agatha Christie. Suspense terrified me.

What an easy target I was in Antigua, with my white skin and chopped yellow hair, with my absurdly awkward baby jogger. No matter how much I loved Olivia, or learned her language and embraced her culture, I would always be an outsider. I scanned the cathedral ruins for hidden cameras. Any storefront could conceal a stake-out.

I came to Santa Lucía, the busy street that separated the

mercado from the rest of Antigua, and ran across. Café Vienna was in the middle of a row of shops on the *mercado's* east side. Set back from the busy street and raised up two steps, the row functioned like a mini stripmall. Customers streamed in and out of the pharmacy, bakery, shoe store, and appliance emporium. Three shoeshiners had set up their chairs at strategic locations.

Cheryl stood in front of Café Vienna, smoking. Her tight white jeans glowed in the mid-morning sun. She was wearing a red striped sailor shirt and white sneakers. Her straight brown hair was pulled back in a ponytail. If not for the creases in her face, she could have passed for a teenager.

When we reached her, she took a long pull and lifted her chin to blow the smoke into the air above our heads.

She jerked her thumb in Olivia's direction. "What a doll," she said without enthusiasm.

"Thank you." My voice quavered.

"Do you have the information?" she asked.

I fumbled in my backpack and produced the piece of paper on which I'd written the information she requested. "This should be everything."

Cheryl squinted at the paper quickly before shoving it into the front pocket of her jeans. She pinched a speck of something off the tip of her tongue while glancing side to side. I was so jumpy I was afraid I might have a heart attack, but Cheryl was as calm as a yoga instructor.

"I have kids available," she said gruffly. "It's only going to get worse. If you want to adopt a brother or sister for your girl, you should do it now."

"I can't imagine adopting again. I just want to finish this one."

"Mary Kay is considering one of my newborns. Cute kid, fat. Another mother is due this weekend."

She raised her eyebrows and turned her face, watching me fish-like from one eye as she inhaled on her cigarette. Two inches of ash smoldered on the end. She gripped the cigarette between two fingers and swung her arm behind her back.

A Guatemalan mother and her daughter walked by. The mother was dressed in a dress and sensible black pumps. The daughter was wearing a plaid skirt and black fuzzy sweater. She was about six years old.

"I didn't want to get involved in all this crap that goes on down here." Cheryl stuck out her lower lip and exhaled. "But you girls have suffered enough."

Suddenly, I heard a shriek. I turned around. The little girl was brushing frantically at her shoulder. The mother was pulling off the girl's sweater. The girl stood in a white cotton undershirt, screaming. Another woman picked up the sweater, which the mother had let drop to the sidewalk. The woman poked her finger through a small hole near the seam at the shoulder. A crowd was beginning to gather.

The shoeshiner closest to Cheryl and me pointed in our direction.

The mother marched toward us, pulling her daughter behind her. She pushed her daughter toward Cheryl and began to yell in Spanish.

Cheryl snubbed out her cigarette with the heel of her white sneaker. "Does she want something?" she asked me coolly. "I don't speak her language."

"She says your cigarette burned her daughter."

Cheryl crossed her arms. "That's ridiculous."

The woman shoved the singed sweater under Cheryl's nose with one hand and shook her daughter's shoulder with the other. "You hurt my daughter!"

The shoeshine man and his client stood up. A few people took a step forward. I leaned in to examine the girl's shoulder. A tiny red circle where the ash must have landed was inscribed on her skin.

I remembered what Kendra had told me about the tourist being attacked by a mob because the crowd thought she was trying to kidnap a baby. Cheryl could have offered the woman money to pay for a new sweater, but that might only have made it worse.

"We need to get out of here." I unlocked the brake on the baby jogger. "It's not safe."

Cheryl didn't delay. Before I knew it, she hopped off the curb and into the street. Her hand was up to hail a passing taxicab.

"I've got kids available," she called out as she pulled the cab door closed. "Think about a little brother."

I dashed with Olivia across the street and merged into the crowd on the opposite sidewalk. My hands were shaking so much I could barely grasp the handlebar on the jogger. I didn't look left or right. I kept walking.

Later that afternoon, I didn't discuss the cigarette incident with Mary Kay when I saw her at the pool with Joaquín. She didn't share the details of her deal, either. It was as though we both knew we were involved with something illicit and slimy, but if we didn't discuss it, it didn't exist. Over the course of the next week, I noticed that Mary Kay was definitely less depressed than she had been, so I figured something must be in the works. I had been to her apartment a month before and was appalled at the chaos. Unmade bed, clothes on the floor, dishes piled in the sink: The classic signs of someone who lacked the energy for any task beyond feeding her baby and changing his diaper. I had stopped seeing her at Conexión and the Fuente Café, but now she was back, checking email and drinking coffee as Joaquín ran around the fountain. She returned to Belli's salon and got her hair cut and highlighted. She was so excited about a red beaded evening bag she had found at the *mercado,* really cheap, that she bought ten of them for Christmas gifts. She exuded the confidence of someone who was going home.

While the two of us had an understanding, it was hard for me to be around the other mothers, especially Kendra. I was afraid I'd accidentally say something about Cheryl. Getting out of PGN was the only subject we mothers ever discussed, and I was usually right there in the conversation. Now I had to be evasive. "It'll happen," I said. "If we're here for Christmas, so be it." I was sure they thought I was odd, because I'd done nothing but complain about our situation for the past four months. Inside, though, my stomach remained in knots. Since I had met with Cheryl, everything was on hold again. Tim and I were just waiting.

Olivia and I were practicing her toddling in the Square when we saw Heather pushing her stroller. "Cheryl is selling babies," Heather said. "Has she called you?"

I put my hands over Olivia's ears.

"I try to avoid any talk about money around Olivia. It's bad enough she hears it from everyone else. She doesn't need to hear it from me."

"But that's what Cheryl's doing." Heather had recently started wearing a khaki hiking hat and dark glasses all the time, the better to hide her magenta hair, I assumed. "She doesn't want to be stuck with a bunch of kids when adoptions shut down again. She's trying to unload them."

"Cheryl mentioned something," I said, not technically lying.

"Just be warned. She's persistent."

Heather pulled her hat down farther on her forehead and pushed off. I didn't tell her that her disguise only made her more obvious. She looked like a cartoon spy.

In two days Tim was due to arrive with the money. I sat under an umbrella on the pool deck feeding Olivia bacon, her current favorite source of protein. I had hoped that Cheryl could arrange to have our case completed when he was in Antigua so we could share the moment together. I imagined us in PGN, standing in Señor Rodríguez's office as he presented us with the signed file. Tim would hug me and I'd lay my head against his chest, both of us crying with relief. But it looked as though I'd receive the file solo.

As I was coaxing Olivia to eat a final bite, I saw Mary Kay walk out of the restaurant, toward us. She was dressed in a long white linen dress, not a swimsuit. She wore turquoise drop earrings and a hammered silver cuff. Instead of Joaquín in her arms, she was carrying an expensive leather handbag. "Come with me into the dressing room," she said. She was taking small, almost mincing steps. She didn't turn around to see if we were following.

No one was paying attention to us. Kendra was in the pool with Susanna. Heather sat on a lounge chair, polishing her toenails. Her husband had arrived and had taken over kid duty, kneeling in the shallow end as he tossed a foam ball. I picked up Olivia and trailed behind Mary Kay past the restaurant, where *carne asada* and red peppers were grilling.

Mary Kay walked over to the bank of showers and pulled aside each curtain. She pushed open each door to the toilet stalls.

I stood in front of the sinks holding Olivia, my throat parched.

Mary Kay's face was grave. "The contact can't trust Cheryl. She wants you to deal with her directly."

I shifted Olivia to my other arm, my mouth open in disbelief. Although I hadn't yet paid Cheryl, I considered her our savior. Now Mary Kay was telling me she was out.

"What happened?"

"The contact said she's talking to too many people."

Mary Kay checked the dressing room door to make sure no one was about to come in. She stood very close to me. "The contact is Belén."

"The attorney's wife? She works at PGN?"

"Her husband has friends inside. They're afraid someone will trace it to him."

I thought of the attorney's wife, well-dressed and prosperous, whom I'd met at the pool. Didn't her husband make enough money without practicing extortion? Even if they demanded payment from only every fifth or sixth family, that was still an exorbitant sum. And while Tim and I could afford another $600, many families couldn't. Not everyone was a physician or investment banker. Teachers and plumbers and carpenters and firefighters adopted children from Guatemala, too.

"What am I supposed to do about Cheryl?"

"Don't talk to her," Mary Kay said. "She can't help you. Belén can help you."

Mary Kay passed me a slip of paper with Belén's number on it. "We got out of PGN this morning."

I was so taken aback, I almost dropped Olivia. "How?"

"I was on speakerphone at Belén's house and a man told us we were out. We took a cab to PGN. Belén went into PGN with an envelope and came back with the file."

"Who did she give the money to?"

"I don't know and I don't care. We'll be home by Christmas."

Our case was more complicated than Mary Kay's. Tim reminded me of that fact when I called him that night with the news. Although the complication seemed minor to us—our *notario* had failed to register the Power of Attorney before he started the adoption—it was regarded as very serious by authorities within PGN. Effectively, our *notario* had acted on our behalf before we'd given him legal permission to do so.

"We don't know if Belén and her contact can fix that," Tim said.

"But Belén got Mary Kay out."

Tim sighed. Getting out of PGN was the only prize that mattered. "Call Belén, then."

I burst into tears.

"Hang in there." Tim's voice was tender. "I'll be there in two days."

When I called Belén at the number Mary Kay gave me, she promised that working around the incorrectly filed Power of Attorney would not be a problem. "We've handled much worse," she assured me, speaking with the quiet assurance of someone who didn't need to raise her voice to be heard. She stressed that her actions were intended to help the children of Guatemala, whom she described as "defenseless."

I didn't ask her why she didn't work to make the system more transparent, then, or to lobby for access to birth control or food stamps. Instead, I thanked her for choosing to help me and Olivia, out of all the Americans who clearly needed her help. We couldn't do this without her.

My cell phone rang as I knelt beside Olivia, bathing her in the small plastic bathtub upstairs. Cheryl's name flashed on caller ID. With trepidation, I pressed the "On" button. Cheryl's fury pounded me like a tidal wave.

"Who's going to get you out of PGN? Me or Mary Kay?"

I thought Belén was going to get us out, but I'd lost track of what the truth was. "You are."

"Who told you to call Belén?"

"I don't remember."

"I have the connection," she snapped. "Not Belén, not Mary Kay."

I heard a match strike. I waited while she took a deep draw. "Belén's husband is a lawyer. You dare to call them at home? He could lose his license. He could lose everything."

Belén must have told Cheryl I called her because Cheryl couldn't have known otherwise. But why? Was Belén angry I called her at home? I was only following Mary Kay's instructions. Was there no one I could trust?

I scooped up a cup of bathwater to rinse the suds from Olivia's hair. She leaned back her head so the water dripped down her back. This simple action of taking care of Olivia, of being her mother, calmed me enough that I could talk to Cheryl.

"I shouldn't have called Belén," I said. "I understand about the chain of command."

"You don't understand one goddamn thing. Not about this country or anything else. And Mary Kay, that rich, selfish bitch. She and that ungrateful husband of hers. I gave them pillows, blankets, and a microwave. I gave them a baby for 14.5 I could've gotten 18 for."

I felt as if I'd been sucker-punched. I was aware that for all their talk about caring for the children of Guatemala, Cheryl and Belén only cared about the money they could leech from the process. But for Cheryl to put an actual price tag on Mary Kay's son was beyond what I ever imagined one human being would do to another.

I was mired in sludge with dishonest people and it felt like an assault. But I couldn't extricate myself. I couldn't risk angering Cheryl. In a month, I would never have to speak to her again. But right now, she held the key to getting us out of here. She had the absolute power.

"Cheryl, I know how much you're trying to help me," I said. "I'm extremely grateful."

"I'm the one with the connection. Don't you forget it."

Chapter 17

THE HOTEL ANTIGUA

Thanksgiving 2003

Although I knew Tim was not due to arrive in Antigua before 7 AM Thanksgiving morning, I was awake most of the night waiting for him. We'd been married twenty-two months and I'd spent the last four of them in Guatemala. I couldn't remember a time when we had discussed any subject not directly related to the adoption. As I thrashed from side to side trying to find a restful position, I worried Tim was not committed to the adoption, but merely humoring me. Granted, he phoned every morning and emailed at night, but my last conscious thought before I finally fell asleep was that perhaps Tim wasn't as devoted to Olivia as I was. If he were, he would have been right beside me, fighting.

At six o'clock I woke to hear the bells tolling in the clock tower and the bus conductor calling all passengers on their way to the capital. "*Guate! Guate!*" The fog hanging over Agua resembled puffs of steam.

The volcano seemed more ominous than usual, and as I sat up in bed, I wondered if today was the day Olivia and I would be covered in ash, preserved Pompeii-like for the ages. Like Agua, our lives seemed to have reached a level of nervous tension.

Tim knocked on the front door at exactly 6:55 AM, as dependable as sunrise.

Although, like me, he'd been up most of the night, he looked refreshed and alert, with no evidence that he had spent the past six hours cramped in a coach seat. My nighttime fears dissipated as he encircled Olivia and me in his arms, pulling us toward him in a bear hug.

"How's my sweetheart?" He ruffled his hand through my short yellow pixie cut. "Nice hair."

I stepped aside in the hallway as he dragged his two large suitcases into the living room. One was packed with cans of formula and jumbo packs of diapers for Olivia, and white T-shirts and blue jeans for me. The other was a treasure trove of books, stuffed animals, and modeling clay. Olivia reached tentatively for a fuzzy white lamb with gingham ears, and a plush gray pig with a pink nose. Tim clapped his encouragement, *ooh*ing and *aah*ing at her discovery of each new goody. He could never have faked that kind of interest.

The feeling was mutual. Within minutes of seeing Tim again, Olivia was literally eating out of his hand. The two of them made cheese omelets for breakfast, to which, I was convinced, Tim must have added some secret ingredient.

"She never eats like that for me," I said as I watched the entire omelet disappear from the tips of Tim's fingers. "It's not fair."

"*Da-da, Da-da*," Olivia called from her high chair, banging on her tray. We were reaping the benefits of Tim's regular phone calls and his patient, one-sided conversations with Olivia. I was thrilled she hadn't forgotten him.

"I was afraid to allow myself to dream this dream," I said. "And here it is, coming true."

Tim smiled and I saw his eyes were misty behind his glasses. "This is the first time we feel like a real family," he said. "The three of us together."

Neither one of us mentioned the $600 in clean bills that Tim had brought. Nor did we confess our fears concerning Cheryl and Belén, and which one of them, if either, we should trust. We refused to formulate a tactic in case the bribe didn't work, or to consider the possibility that the adoption could have dragged on long enough that Ana might change her mind.

After breakfast, I stacked the dishes in the sink as Tim carried Olivia piggyback around the dining room table. They climbed the stairs while counting to ten. He bounced her on his knees and warbled "The Noble Duke of York." Tim turned on the CD player and I heard them in the living room dancing salsa to the music of Carlos Santana. If ten years before someone had told me that someday I would stand in my kitchen in Guatemala while my husband and daughter danced salsa to Santana, I never would have believed them.

I called my parents in San Diego, where the rest of my family had gathered for Thanksgiving, and talked to everyone on speaker-phone. My sisters and brother had exhausted every possible connection they had, but they remained positive.

"It has to happen," Patrice said.

"Don't give up," my brother added.

"How're the language classes?" Adrienne asked. "Are you *habla-ing* in *español?*"

"*Absolutamente.*"

My sister, Deanna, told me her three daughters had written and illustrated a book welcoming Olivia to the family. My youngest niece got on the phone.

"Is your baby coming home soon?" she asked.

"I hope so," I answered.

The Hotel Antigua was serving a Thanksgiving dinner with turkey and the traditional sides. All the adoptive families in Antigua were going. I put on Olivia's red corduroy dress and white leather oxfords and wore the fitted tan trousers I had bought to wear to PGN. Tim wore a pressed white shirt with dress pants and his brown-and-green cornucopia tie.

Before we left, I suggested we take a short detour to the Cathe-dral to inquire about baptizing Olivia. Yolanda had promised Olivia would be baptized at some point during the process. The fact that I had believed her seemed ludicrous now, an indication of how gullible I'd been. But talking to my family—especially my father—reminded me of how our shared religious traditions were an essential part of the glue that held us together. I wasn't sure if I believed in the need for a baby to be cleansed of "original sin," but I didn't want to take any chances. Olivia was a member of our family, too. I wanted her to receive the sacrament before we got on a plane to return home.

Baptisms took place one Sunday a month, in an outdoor grotto in the sprawling ruins behind the Cathedral. A huge crowd of mostly indigenous families gathered. The men dressed in their best white shirts. The women wore shawls over their heads with threads so bright the shaded grotto seemed illuminated. The priest blessed the baby and dunked her head in a *pila bautismal*—baptismal font—filled with holy water as the godparents, *los padrinos*, stood by.

The young man behind the desk at the Cathedral office seemed baffled by our request. If we were, as we claimed, Olivia's parents, we should have had a birth certificate. We did not. Nor could we supply the names and baptismal certificates of *los padrinos*. He shook his head. We would have to wait until the adoption was final.

"Can I at least show my husband the *pila bautismal?*" I asked.

"*Claro, claro.*" He waved us toward the grotto in the back.

Even in daylight, and without the women's bright shawls, the setting felt dark and sacred. This, I knew, was a holy place.

"Can't we baptize her here, ourselves?" I said. "You can do that in emergencies. With only a drop of water."

Tim walked over to the *pila*. "A drop is about what's in here."

I handed Olivia over to Tim and dipped two fingers into the holy water before inscribing a cross over Olivia's forehead. "I baptize you in the name of the Father, and of the Son, and of the Holy Spirit. Amen." I bowed my head as Olivia let out a single, questioning yelp. "Now it's official."

"Alleluia," Tim said. "At least something is."

Every American living in Guatemala must have been eating Thanksgiving dinner at Hotel Antigua. The restaurant was filled with faces I'd never seen before: middle-aged hippies, retired expats, students, backpackers, and missionaries. Guatemalans were dining, too, but the air crackled with the sound of English, so loud it almost drowned out the lively melodies of the marimba combo performing on the pool deck. As crowded as the restaurant was, though, it was easy to spot the adoptive moms. They were the white women with the brown babies. Not only did they fill the longest table in the restaurant, they were also making the most noise. In addition to the Antigua moms, four others had come in for the day from the capital. The hostess had wisely placed our group in the corner nearest the marimba combo.

Kendra raised an arm to signal me when we arrived. I hardly

recognized her in a sage green dress and jade necklace. She was seated in the middle of the table, with Susanna in a high chair beside her.

"You must be Tim." She smiled as she scooted in her chair so we could get by. "I won't ask you about Susanna's rash until after dinner."

After I'd known Kendra for a month, I confessed to her that when we first met I'd worried she was only nice to me for easy access to medical advice. Now that we were close friends, she liked to kid me about it.

I patted her shoulder as I passed. "Green's your color," I said. I was feeling a little disloyal about not telling her of our arrangement with Cheryl and Belén, but Tim and I had agreed not to tell anyone, even our families.

Because there were no high chairs left, Tim held Olivia on his lap. I sat across from them.

"This is quite a group," Tim said. He stood up halfway as I introduced him to Heather and her husband, and their daughter, Isabella. The rest of the table was filled with other adoptive families I had just met. "How many of you are there?"

"Two less than yesterday," Heather said. "Ruby and Catherine just got out of PGN. Did you hear?"

I shot Tim a look across the table and he nodded once to show me he understood. We were to say nothing.

Kendra reached for the basket of tortillas in the center of the table. "Ruby deserved to get out. She's a pediatric cardiologist. And Catherine has ten other kids at home, five of them adopted. A few have special needs."

Heather scowled. "That's nice they're so wonderful. But we all deserve to get out."

I sometimes forgot how young Heather was: barely out of her teens. She looked as though she might cry. "Remember," I said. "You're with your baby. So many parents aren't."

Heather pressed her lips together resolutely. "I know," she said. "You're right."

But I understood how Heather felt. As glad as we were that Ruby and Catherine were going home, our joy was subdued. We were the wallflowers in high school who nobody asked to dance. Overlooked and left behind. We wanted to go home, too.

Heather folded a tortilla and took a bite. "Ruby had it wired," she said between chews. "I heard she paid for her birth mother to get vitamins and medical care before the kid was born."

"I thought you could only do that in the States," Kendra said.

"You can do it here with the right agency. You have to pay extra. Most of these girls know they're not keeping the baby."

Kendra and I frowned at each other, wondering how we'd allowed ourselves to miss that opportunity. We would have paid almost any amount to provide prenatal care. Thanksgiving dinner suddenly felt less festive.

"Do we serve ourselves?" Tim asked. He placed his napkin beside his plate before swinging Olivia onto his hip and heading for the buffet.

"Who was Ruby's *notario*?" Kendra asked Heather.

"Vargas."

"No wonder." Kendra reached for another tortilla. "He's the best."

I felt guilty that I was pretending to agree, but I used to believe that the best *notarios* were the ones who were smarter and worked harder, too. Now I was sure they were the ones who understood whom to pay off. Not wanting to contribute to the conversation, I excused myself from the table to follow Tim to the buffet line. I found him zeroed in on a chafing dish filled with stuffing made from tortillas instead of corn bread. In broken Spanish, he was asking the server if the chef was willing to share the recipe.

A pale-skinned man behind me motioned toward Olivia, who was clinging to Tim's waist with her legs.

"Is she your daughter?"

"She is," I said, after a very slight hesitation. "From Totonicapán."

I didn't know why I was compelled to add this information, except that the man looked as if he might have known where Toto was. I nudged Tim so he would turn around. If this was a conversation I didn't want to have, Tim could be my reinforcement.

"I was watching your group." The man indicated the long table of Americans. "Of all of the children, she's the most purely indigenous. The long, narrow face, the flat nose, the almond-shaped eyes. She looks like a Mayan princess."

Tim chucked Olivia under her chin with his free hand. "Thank you. We think so."

The man pulled out his wallet from his front pocket and handed me a business card.

"I work with a mission group in the highlands. We often have girls in the villages who want to put up their babies for adoption. Cases of rape, incest. Girls too young to get married."

I glanced down at the man's card: John T. Woods. The organization was one I'd never heard of. I slipped the card into my back pocket. "We're not really interested at the moment."

"But if in the future."

He smiled at Tim and me before drifting toward a woman on the other end of the buffet line who appeared to be his wife. I watched as he said something to her and gestured in our direction. When her eyes lit on us, she lifted her palm in a friendly wave.

"Was he trying to s-e-l-l us a baby?" Tim said, spelling the word as I nodded at the woman across the room. He hoisted Olivia higher up his hip and jiggled her gently. "Solicited while waiting for tortilla stuffing."

"You learn a lot when you live here," I said. "Sometimes more than you want to know."

When we returned to the table, Kendra's jaw was set at a hard angle, and her face was blotchy and red. Heather was leaning forward with both elbows on the table, jabbing at the air with her right index finger to emphasize her statements.

I'd only seen Kendra this upset once before, and that was when she talked about her friend in the Peace Corps who'd ended up with his head on a pole.

"I know this country better than you do," Kendra was saying. "You cannot bribe PGN."

"But people *are* bribing PGN," Heather countered. "Everybody knows it: Some random American dad stood up in the U.S. Embassy and announced it. 'PGN is taking bribes.' He said if you didn't cooperate you would never get out, and that's why he's stuck here. He wanted to know what the Embassy was going to do about it."

"So the only people who get out are people who pay bribes?" Kendra said the word "bribes" as though it were poison. "You think Ruby and Catherine paid bribes? What about Mary Kay? She got out last week. Did she pay a bribe?"

"How do I know what they did?" Heather opened her palms toward Kendra, as if to prove her innocence. "I'm only telling you what I heard. An American dad told the Embassy PGN was taking bribes."

I concentrated on keeping my face blank. The Embassy may have ignored whatever was happening in PGN in the past, claiming that the U.S. had no jurisdiction there, but the Embassy couldn't turn a blind eye now, not when Americans were being forced to commit crimes in order to complete their adoptions. Under such intense scrutiny by the U.S., the bribery within PGN would have to stop. Or at least pause for a few months until the issue blew over. The question of whom to trust—Cheryl or Belén—was a moot one.

Neither one of them could help us now.

I pulled out my chair, sat down, and opened my napkin across my lap. Across from me, Tim was listening so intently, he didn't notice that the sleeve of Olivia's white turtleneck was dipped in his mashed potatoes. His face looked unruffled, but I could tell from the tautness of his neck muscles that this conversation had knocked him sideways, the same as it had for me.

I stared at Tim until I got his attention, and when I did, I felt his shoe brush up against my calf under the table. He was trying to get me to calm down. I sank the tines of my fork into the tortilla stuffing.

We may not have been able to pay a bribe, but we still had Señor Rodríguez. He was the one who'd tracked down our *notario* and called him personally to get us an appointment. Rodríguez had told me about Olivia's first foster mother when he didn't have to. He insisted I call him *Miguel*. Rodríguez knew how devoted I was to Olivia. Rodríguez would help us.

Kendra turned her attention to me. "You go to PGN all the time. Have you noticed anything suspicious going on?"

"Never," I said. "Not a hint."

I felt Heather's eyes boring through me. "What do you do there?" Heather asked. "Do you meet with someone?"

"I sit around in the waiting room a lot." I forced a laugh. "You know how it is. The girls at the reception desk know me very well."

"Have you been upstairs?"

"I've *seen* the stairs leading to the second floor, but I've never gone up them. I'm too focused on pleading my case downstairs. I meet with Miguel Rodríguez in his office. Next to the lobby."

I felt a tiny bit smug when I said *Miguel Rodríguez,* knowing that I was the only one of the moms on a first-name basis with him.

Heather fluttered her fingers as though brushing away a mosquito. "Miguel Rodríguez." She made a dismissive sound. "He's a mid-level pencil pusher. If you don't go upstairs to the chief's office, you're wasting your time."

I stared at her to see if she was joking. "I thought Rodríguez was in charge."

"Rodríguez is a gatekeeper. A nobody. His power is exactly this." Heather touched her index finger to her thumb. "Zero."

The room was still noisy with conversation and music, but the sounds were drowned out by an explosion inside my head. I didn't think I could do this anymore. I couldn't keep fighting. The volcano was erupting and I was under it.

Later that night, after we'd read *A Mother for Choco* and *Tell Me Again About the Night I Was Born,* when Olivia was finally asleep, Tim and I tiptoed to the bedroom downstairs. I moved onto the floor

the bags of *típica* and collection of paintings I stored on the double
bed. Tim closed the door. As I straightened up, he pulled down the
strap of my nightgown. Reflexively, I pulled away.

"I'm sorry," I said. I knew I sounded irritated.

Tim pulled me toward him. "I'm upset, too," he murmured
into my neck. "But we can't do anything about it now." The length
of his body pressed closer to mine. "Let's be in the moment and
enjoy each other." He edged us closer to the bed, and we fell onto
it. "Try to relax."

I felt a rush of cold air as he sat up to pull off his undershirt,
then warmth again as he lay beside me. He kissed me deeply. I understood that he was aching for me, and that I should have been aching
for him, too. But I was imagining the scene in the U.S. Embassy, the
disgruntled father who blew the whistle on PGN. Had he stopped to
consider what his revelation might have done to the rest of us?

To have paid a bribe would have been foolhardy, insane.

I tried to shift my focus to Tim's mouth on my breast. If I could
have just given myself over to it, I would have been a lot more relaxed.
But I couldn't stop replaying Heather's scathing assessment of
Rodríguez. Even as she spoke, I knew what she said was true. He was
too nice, too available, to have been a person of any real influence.
I had met with him at least a dozen times and he had accomplished
nothing. We were as stuck as we ever were. How could I have been
such an idiot?

Tim lifted up my hips and slipped my nightgown down past my feet. He retrieved it from under the covers, tossed it onto the floor. I turned my head sideways and reviewed every document in our file as he moved above me. The birth, marriage, and divorce certificates; the fingerprint clearances and home study; the medical reports and reference letters; the tax returns from the past three years. Everything was notarized, stamped by Sacramento, approved by the Guatemalan consulate in San Francisco. What else did they want?

I threw a sheet over Tim as he curled up beside me in sleep. I stroked his damp hair back from his forehead and stared at the ceiling.

Chapter 18

OUT

In my backpack, I carried a bottle of water, three energy bars, my passport, my wallet, my phone, and tissues because by midday the restroom would be out of toilet paper.

A gardener was hunched over the raised flower beds that formed the letters "PGN." I opened the double front doors. One of the receptionists was peering into a small hand mirror and plucking her eyebrows. The other chatted with one of the dashing male attorneys I saw during my every visit, blinking *ojitos* at his comments. The female guard buzzed me through the door marked *ENTRADA* without glancing at my passport. I peeked through the office window where I caught sight of Rodríguez at his desk, white shirt rolled up at the sleeves as his gold bracelet slid around his thin wrist. He was talking to a woman sitting on his sofa, and although I barely made out her silhouette, I sensed she was an American adoption agency owner there to discuss her clients. I didn't think Rodríguez saw me, or if he did, he chose not to acknowledge my presence. I didn't mind, because it was not Rodríguez I'd come to see.

I was going upstairs, to the chief's office.

My plan was to discover the exact status of our case. If he said we needed something easy, like the good manners letter or updated letters of recommendation, I'd tell him I could get those things, but could he promise me that would be the end of the *previos*? And if he said we needed something complicated—and I wasn't sure what that might be—I'd tell him my daughter needed her father and I needed my husband. I'd remind him Christmas was coming. I'd talk for as long as he would listen. I'd wait eight hours if I had to. I'd stay until they threw me out.

I walked up the stairs, grasping the railing with my right hand as if I knew where I was going. At the top, I hesitated, trying to decide where to go next. The offices on my left seemed to deal with geological surveys or zoning regulations—the walls were covered with maps. The ones on the right were labeled *LICENCIADOS*, which I believed referred to the lawyers who reviewed adoptions.

A woman with very short hair wearing a pantsuit and stilettos came clicking up behind me. Fearful she might have asked me what business I had, I turned right. Long fluorescent tubes flickered and twitched on the dropped ceiling. I saw one window, which overlooked the street-level parking lot.

A young man behind a metal typing desk in the reception area pushed back his chair. "May I help you?"

It took me a moment to realize he was Lorenzo, the translator for Señor Rodríguez so many months ago. I hadn't expected to run into him upstairs—hadn't considered what might happen if someone who knew me saw me.

I returned his politely limp handshake. "Here I am again." I shrugged sheepishly. "Oh well."

If I told him I was upstairs to find the chief, he might have perceived me as criticizing Rodríguez and everyone else downstairs. My eyes lit again on the word LICENCIADOS. The perfect excuse.

"I would like to speak with my reviewer, if possible," I said. "I believe Señor Rodríguez said her name is Rivera?"

He looked past me toward an office at the end of the hall.

"I must confirm her identity," Lorenzo said. "Before I may proceed."

He stepped over to the desk beside him and opened a leather-bound ledger, flipping through a few pages. "Your name again, please?"

"Berger." I pronounced it with the Guatemalan soft "g." "Like the president."

He ran his finger down the page. "*Sí, sí.* Berger. Excuse me."

He didn't so much walk down the hallway toward the *licenciada*'s office as he strutted.

The reception area was empty. I edged closer to the leather-bound ledger on the desk beside Lorenzo's. As in Family Court, columns of names were entered neatly in black pen, some with information filled in across the page, others only halfway.

This time, I found our names easily because our listing had a red asterisk beside it. Did this mark us as having an arrangement with Cheryl? Or was it because something was so wrong with our case it needed further scrutiny? I was still staring at it when Lorenzo returned.

"*Licenciada* Rivera can meet with you only if you have an appointment," he said.

I felt his eyes on my back as I returned to the hallway. When I reached the wide central staircase, I pretended to begin my slow descent. One step, two steps. Below me on the first floor, female clerks scurried from office to office toting files, as a *muchacha* carrying a basket of tortillas made her mid-morning rounds. The shoeshiner was buzzed in clutching his square wooden shoeshine kit. And somewhere in this vast building, Olivia's file languished along with the files of the rest of the children awaiting adoption.

I lingered briefly. Changed direction.

I climbed back upstairs and turned left, toward the offices with the maps. When a few people who looked like lawyers passed me the other way, I studied my wristwatch. I continued walking down a long, wide hallway, toward what I hoped was the chief's office.

The blue-and-white flag of Guatemala was planted in an iron base in the corner of a small waiting area. A row of five chairs, lined against the wall, led up to a narrow Plexiglas window that acted as a barrier to the receptionist's desk. A man and a woman, each with a briefcase between their feet, sat in the chairs, waiting. The man was older and white, in a green boiled-wool jacket that seemed more suited to the Bavarian Alps than Central America. The woman was middle-aged and olive-skinned, in a tightly fitting red suit. Her gold sandals had ankle straps and four-inch heels. She was wearing red eyeglasses. I recognized her as the Guatemalan attorney Tim and I had seen months ago during one of our desperate forays to the U.S. Embassy. She was the one with the thick binder, holding the hands of another American couple as they waited for their pink slip. Here she was again, unbelievably.

I had expected the chief's office to be grander than Rodríguez's, but it was of the same shabby vintage. The telephone on the receptionist's desk was so old it had a dial. I didn't see a computer.

Acting as though it was totally reasonable for me to be upstairs in PGN, I greeted the receptionist and haltingly explained my situation. I heard "next week" and "impossible." As I tried to formulate my response, the receptionist indicated she couldn't understand my Spanish and pushed open her window an inch or two wider.

"Sofía," she said without preamble. "*Por favor.*" She asked the woman in the red suit to translate.

"I saw you at the Embassy," I said.

Sofía's head barely moved, but she indicated that, yes, she was the lawyer who had been at the Embassy. She was also the lawyer who presented her clients' cases upstairs in the chief's office, instead of expecting them to magically complete themselves, unassisted. She grasped me in a light hug. "The people in this office will not help you," she whispered in English. Then, in a conversational tone she said, "Sit beside me and tell me what you need."

I was afraid that the man in the boiled-wool jacket might speak English and have overheard our conversation. But he was studying the pages of a small, dog-eared notebook and seemed not to notice us.

My cell phone rang from the depths of my backpack.

Flustered, I dug through my papers. "Mary Kay" read the name on the display. As far as I knew, Mary Kay had moved back to the Camino Real to await her Embassy appointment and pink slip. Why would she be calling? I thrust the phone back in my bag. It stopped ringing only long enough to go into voicemail. Rang again. I fished it out. Mary Kay. What could she possibly want?

The phone rang a third time. I held down the power button to turn it off. Mary Kay would have to wait.

Sofía patted the chair beside her, casually crossing her legs. Gazing straight ahead, she continued to speak. "Give me your case number. I have a friend in the office who will show me the file."

I was reluctant to call more attention to our asterisked file, but what else could I do? Sofía excused herself, loudly and in Spanish, to go to the ladies' room. I watched her pass the flags and disappear down the hallway toward the reviewer's office.

But it was a voice directly beside me that said: "Welcome to the tropics."

The white man beside me grinned. His long, narrow teeth were stained yellow.

"You speak English?" I asked.

"And German and French and Italian. Spanish, *por supuesto.*" He draped his arm over the back of the seat where Sofía had sat, his eyes gleeful as he recited the list.

"I realize I'm at a distinct disadvantage not speaking Spanish well."

"Your Spanish is fine." His voice was thick with a German accent. "They can't help you anyway." He tapped Sofía's chair. "She can, maybe. But the others." He wagged his foot toward the receptionist's office. "You go over their heads. This is the way business is done."

I cleared my throat, glancing down the hallway for Sofía. I wasn't sure if the man was a crackpot or someone who might know something. In his boiled-wool jacket, he looked like a Tyrolean yodeler.

"Sounds like you've been around for a while," I said. "What do you do here?"

"I help people like you. Last week it was an American they accused of kidnapping her own baby. She flew home." He sighed. "The baby stayed behind."

I felt my face harden. Real or imagined, losing the baby was always the threat. No other system could manipulate parents to the same degree as the bureaucracy of Guatemalan adoption. I added the Tyrolean yodeler to my growing list of people who profited from the adoption business, although I was not sure in which category to place him or what I would ever do with the list.

"You must get a lot of American clients just waiting outside this office," I said.

"Only desperate people make it this far. You, Señora Berger, are one of a few."

I didn't know whether to be honored or insulted. In either case, I didn't want to give him the satisfaction of witnessing my anxiety. I made a big show of burrowing through my backpack for my cell phone and powering it on.

The strategy seemed to work. He stood up so sharply, I almost expected him to salute. "Call me if you need me. My rates are reasonable."

Pressing my phone to my ear, I waved distractedly. Six new messages.

"Jessica, this is Mary Kay. I need to talk to you."

"Jessica, please pick up the phone."

"Jessica. I know you're there. This is Mary Kay."

My phone rang. I answered without checking the incoming number.

"Mary Kay?"

"This is Cheryl. Get the hell out of PGN. They know what you're up to."

The receptionist was not at her desk. The hallway was empty. I cupped my hand over the mouthpiece. "Who?"

"Are you that stupid? Get the hell out." She hung up.

"Señora Berger." Sofía appeared at the end of the hallway, tee-tering toward me on her gold sandals. Under her arm she carried our manila file.

"Where did you get this?" I asked, panicked.

"I have friends." She settled onto her chair and opened the file on her lap. "It is as I suspected. Your *notario* is not good." Her voice drifted off. "Your papers are a mess."

She flipped to the back for the summary letter from the reviewer. "They want the new medicals, birth certificate, and the police report."

"Everything," I interrupted her. "They want everything."

I reached over to close the folder, but she was holding it tightly in her hands.

"Somebody's watching me," I said. "They're afraid I'm here to expose them. They called my friend from Antigua."

Sofía closed the folder and slipped it into her briefcase. She handed me a business card and told me to meet her at her office in two hours.

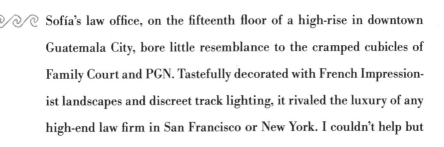 Sofía's law office, on the fifteenth floor of a high-rise in downtown Guatemala City, bore little resemblance to the cramped cubicles of Family Court and PGN. Tastefully decorated with French Impression-ist landscapes and discreet track lighting, it rivaled the luxury of any high-end law firm in San Francisco or New York. I couldn't help but

wonder if her adoption practice had paid for such sumptuous digs, or if the profits came from some other area of law. Whatever her source of income, Sofía was very successful.

The secretary said Sofía was on her way and directed me to the lobby, where four young pregnant girls and obvious foster mothers with babies were sprawled on sofas upholstered in black-and-white toile. I felt as if I were back at the Camino Real hotel, except everyone was Guatemalan, and four of the babies hadn't been born yet. One of the foster mothers explained they were waiting for the pediatrician to arrive for his monthly visit. Sofía had discovered it was more efficient for the doctor to come to her office than for her to shuttle the girls and babies to him. They were all snacking on take-out boxes of Pollo Campero, so I assumed lunch was part of the lure to keep the appointment.

Sofía swept in carrying her briefcase, pausing to kiss each baby and ask each pregnant girl how she was feeling. Her concern and affection for each one of them was so real that I understood why they had chosen her to handle their adoptions. Given a choice, I imagined anyone would have. Sofía explained that I was an adoptive mother from California, but not to any of their babies. I felt uneasy as they inspected me from head to toe, as if I were a rare species they'd heard about but never seen.

Sofía's corner office was dominated by an almost life-size oil portrait of Sofía, her husband, and two young girls Sofía identified as her daughters. The picture window behind her vast, glass-topped desk overlooked the downtown skyline. A light rap on the door announced the receptionist, who padded in with two cups of coffee and a carafe of steamed milk. Sofía remained silent while the receptionist prepared a cup for each of us and backed out of the room.

After the door was closed, Sofía spoke. "Here in Guatemala, we have protocols. We take very seriously the manner in which documents are prepared. The dates on which they are filed. The position and timeliness of an official seal. Who signed what and when."

We both knew Tim's and my *notario*, Simón Guerrero, had waited almost a year before filing our Power of Attorney. His negligence had led to a chain of events that felt like a life sentence. Papers had been filed out of order. What did Sofía expect from me? I couldn't change the past.

"Señor Rodríguez holds you in great esteem," Sofía said. "Because of this, he has agreed to be of assistance."

I was afraid to breathe. Did Rodríguez have power to help me, or didn't he? First, I thought did, until Heather convinced me he didn't.

Sofía explained that as Secretary General, Señor Rodríguez assigned each case to a reviewer. Each reviewer was different. Some had sympathy to adopting parents. Some did not. Some imposed many *previos*. Some imposed none.

"It's a roll of the dice," Sofía said, "which one you get."

PGN should not have filed the case without a Power of Attorney.

But because it did, PGN implied its consent. It indicated that the case was acceptable. What Rodríguez could do was change the reviewer to one who understood that PGN created the initial problem. The new reviewer would examine the paperwork and approve it. The chief would sign off on Friday.

I gripped the arms of my chair in disbelief. It seemed impossible that after nearly two years of fighting for Olivia, the battle was almost over. I couldn't permit myself to be hopeful again, not if it meant being disappointed. "What's the catch?" I asked. There had to be something.

Sofía paused briefly, almost as if she were embarrassed by what she was about to say. "Are you willing to thank Rodríguez with a small gift?"

I remembered his old laptop, held together with duct tape. "A new computer?"

She shook her head. "Nothing too big."

"A gold pen?"

Her eyes brightened. "Perfect."

My mind was already in the stationery store in Antigua where I knew I could buy one. It was handsome, but not too expensive. Something he wouldn't buy for himself.

"For the new reviewer, too?" I said. "Also a pen?"

She nodded her agreement

"And you?" I said to Sofía. "What would you like?"

She pressed her lips together. "Someday someone will be kind to my children," she said. "For me, that is enough."

As Juan Carlos drove me to PGN, my melancholy surprised me. I should have been ecstatic that our ordeal was almost over, that Olivia would be ours officially, that we were finally going home. But as we chugged up the hill out of Antigua and toward Guatemala City, I only felt a kind of numb detachment. I remembered the first time I had made this trip five months earlier, with my realtor, Nadine, giving me a brief Antigua history, and a nervous, pensive Olivia in the backseat. We had just bid a tearful goodbye to Lupe and the Garza family, and I was wracked with guilt over the pain I had inflicted on all of them because I was participating in an adoption that went on for too long, for reasons beyond my control. And the part of me that didn't feel guilty had been consumed by fear—of Yolanda and Theodore and how they might harm us, of our *notario* and the entire adoption process, of living in a foreign country. I was a different person now. My old self no longer existed.

Kendra and I were the only two mothers still in Antigua. Catherine and Ruby had left before Thanksgiving. Mary Kay was now living at the Camino Real, waiting for her pink slip. I hadn't seen Heather for a few days, and when I did, she announced she was out of PGN and moving to the capital. She may have worked out an arrangement with Cheryl or Belén, I didn't know. She left without saying goodbye. Twelve-year-old Dorothy remained with her vendor-mother, Rose. Nadine had segued from renting houses to facilitating adoptions. Partnering with a lawyer from Michigan, she opened an agency whose marketing materials touted the fact that Nadine lived in Guatemala and understood the country. She was such a savvy businesswoman, her shift from real estate to adoptions was inevitable. The commissions were probably bigger.

Soon after Cheryl had met me in the *mercado* and burned the little Guatemalan girl's sweater, two thugs roughed her up. One pushed her down and kicked her in the ribs while the other rifled through her pocketbook and stole her wallet and passport. The episode had scared Cheryl enough that she left Antigua two days later, staying long enough only to pack up her belongings and make flight arrangements. No one had heard from her since.

I worried about Kendra. Her lawyer had received no response to his newspaper notices seeking the fathers of birth mother Febi's ten siblings. Nor did he expect to. There was very little else, legally, to be done. I had no doubt Kendra would do whatever it took to adopt Susanna, even if that meant falsifying Febi's birth certificate so she appeared older. Otherwise, Kendra would have to wait two years until Febi turned eighteen and was able to thumbprint the relinquishment herself.

I wished that Tim were with me to share my last trip to PGN, a triumphant final lap. Despite our moments of tension, he had been my stalwart partner, unswerving in his dedication to adopting Olivia. As I watched the green blur of Antigua forest dissolve into the gray landscape of the capital, I reminded myself that he'd be here for our Embassy appointment, when the U.S. government issued us our pink slip and we were allowed to go home.

Being together at that final stage would have to be enough.

Sofía rushed through PGN's double front doors and hugged me. Beside her was Simón Guerrero's assistant, Gilda. Sofía said the file must be checked out to the *notario* or his assistant, who would procure the Guatemalan passport and birth certificate and submit the file to the U.S. Embassy for the pink slip. When I protested, saying how afraid I was that Gilda would lose the file, Sofía said it had to be done this way.

"Rodríguez will be watching," were Sofía's exact words. "Gilda will do the work and hold onto the file."

Gilda also hugged me as though we were old friends. As insincere as it felt, I returned her embrace with an air-kiss. What else could I do?

Sofía had told me not to buy her anything, but I did: a deep red amulet and earrings intended to coordinate with the striking red suits she wore whenever I saw her. Without a second glance at the matching set, she thrust it into her briefcase as if to deny the exchange ever occurred. I hoped I hadn't offended her.

Together, we passed the two receptionists on their cell phones and the guard who waved us in without glancing up from her magazine. Rodríguez was behind his desk, typing furiously on his laptop. The gray duct tape still held the machine together, but I couldn't guess how much longer it would last.

The new reviewer was tall and thin. His black eyeglass frames were narrow and stylish, the kind of glasses worn by designers and architects. He was somber and silent, probably in his mid-thirties. I didn't catch his name.

Without any fanfare or discussion, Rodríguez showed me the file. He directed me to the final page, where the chief had signed and approved it. I had imagined I might throw my arms up over my head and scream, or dance around the middle of the room and turn cartwheels. Instead, I inspected the last page in silence, and thanked the four of them for their help. I promised to take good care of Olivia.

I handed Rodríguez two gold pens, one for him and one for the reviewer. Then, before anyone could change his mind, I walked out of PGN for the last time.

Chapter 19

PINK SLIP

"Your fingerprints have expired," Mandy Márquez said from behind Door #8 of the Embassy. "You'll have to go back to California to get new ones."

"Aren't fingerprints forever?" I asked.

"Not in international adoption. They're only good for fifteen months."

I was afraid there'd be something. Tim had gotten our home study updated, which had also expired, but now I needed fingerprints.

Olivia stirred on my lap. She and I had stood in line at the Embassy since five in the morning to see Márquez. It was a few minutes before noon.

I tried to keep my voice even. "I'd really prefer not to go back to California until this is finished. Isn't there anyone in Guatemala qualified to make a new set?"

Mandy Márquez's eyes darted over to Olivia and back to me. In the six months since we first met Márquez, Olivia had doubled in size. "One of our Guatemalan employees. He only takes prints on Monday afternoons from two until three."

"I'll be there," I said.

On Monday, we made a second pilgrimage to the Embassy. I recognized the man who greeted me to take my fingerprints. I'd seen him managing the line of people waiting to enter the Embassy. He led me into the area where visitors check their cameras and cell phones, and had their backpacks searched. Hundreds of Guatemalans were lined up, waiting to go inside to petition the Embassy for visas. A few dozen close to us watched as the man opened his briefcase on the counter and pulled out a stamp pad. As I tried to keep Olivia beside me, he picked up my right thumb and wiped it with a square soaked in alcohol, then dried it with a cotton ball before rolling it in ink and pressing it firmly on a piece of white cardboard. Before proceeding to my ring finger, he waited for the ink to dry.

This felt like a ten-minute job that he would stretch to sixty minutes, but I knew better than to rush him. Let him work at his own pace. I answered pleasantly as he asked me the usual questions about Olivia, aware that the petitioners waiting in line were also listening. Yes, she was mine. Yes, she was adopted. From Totonicapán.

Olivia scooted under the counter, bored by the wait, and from somewhere, discovered a pencil. Except I didn't know she had a pencil until I picked her up to stop her from running around, and she managed to maneuver the pencil onto the white cardboard displaying my prints and mark it with a faint pencil line. Could a line as thin as a spiderweb ruin everything? I looked at the man's face, but he seemed unconcerned. It had been such a grueling day already, coming in from Antigua and wrangling Olivia, and the man was finally pressing down on my left pinky. I couldn't bear the thought of starting over.

A week later, Márquez called me on my cell phone. "Bad news," she said. "There was a problem with the prints."

For my second round of prints, I left Olivia at home with Aracely and Junior. Olivia didn't object; she and Junior were old pals, so much so that I worried over how much she would miss him when we left. Another person who disappeared from her young life, like Lupe. I still felt guilty about our meeting in the Square, about not inviting Lupe back to visit. I debated whether I should before we left for good.

When I arrived at the Embassy, the fingerprint man was waiting with his stamp pad and briefcase. "My prints are never rejected," he said, as if he couldn't understand the outcome himself. "I am called the best."

Solemnly, he rolled my fingertips across the ink pad and pressed them onto the cardboard. The sample was pristine.

Antigua was preparing for Christmas. Not with holiday decorations and before-Christmas sales, but with two solid weeks of parades that highlighted performances on one instrument: the drums. Morning and afternoon, hundreds of uniformed school children marched through the streets pounding on kettles, snares, and tom-toms, and banging on cymbals and tambourines. From kindergarteners to high school seniors, every child from the surrounding region was thumping on something percussive. The whole city vibrated and shook. Grown-ups dressed as cartoon characters I'd never seen before—Fuzzy Fox, Miss Mittens, *El Oso Gordo*—formed a conga line behind the drummers. Grocery store clerks tossing out laundry soap samples brought up the rear. Olivia and I clapped and swayed along with a thousand other spectators on the steps of the Cathedral and *Municipalidad*. Guatemala claimed the marimba as its national instrument, but in Antigua, drums ruled. The celebration felt like Carnival and Mardi Gras rolled into one.

On December 12, Tim wire-transferred $10,000 to Yolanda's bank account, our balance due. Despite how little she had done for us, we never considered *not* paying her. An agreement was an agreement, even if Yolanda never held up her end of the bargain. I took Olivia to Antigua's *Municipalidad*, where I procured copies of the new version of her birth certificate, naming Tim and me as her mother and father. Gilda met us in the capital for Olivia's Guatemalan passport, necessary for her to enter the United States, where she was legally identified as "Berger O'Dwyer." Although the *notario*, Simón Guerrero, was not present, the attorney, or *mandatario*, was. A specialist in litigation, he simply signed off on adoptions to make extra money. Like Guerrero, the *mandatorio* was younger than I was, and dressed in a blue three-piece suit. Suspended across his vest was an antique watch fob. He had never heard of me, Tim, or Olivia. He claimed not to know Yolanda or Theodore.

Before we started Olivia's adoption, I would have shaken the *mandatorio*'s hand and said something polite and obsequious. But today I looked him in the eye and asked, "Did you know that my daughter's adoption took more than a year? Do you have any idea how disrupted her life has been?"

The *mandatorio* pulled on his watch fob and checked the time, before letting it drop with a shrug. Theodore had been right. Nobody cared.

Olivia and I were walking to Conexión to check email when Mandy Márquez called.

"Are you sitting down?" she asked.

I set Olivia down in a doorway, standing to block her from the sidewalk traffic. "What's up?"

"Your fingerprints have been lost." She waited for me to gasp before she explained. "The print man sent two sets, yours and another American's. I saw him pack them up, both in the same envelope. The second set arrived safely and has been approved." Márquez sighed. "Yours are gone. I can't believe it myself."

Olivia nudged herself against my legs and raised her arms for me to pick her up. I felt as if I were submerged in quicksand, flailing for something to hold onto. The U.S. government allowed only two months to elapse between the time a case was released by PGN and the final pink slip was issued. If the subsequent paperwork took more than two months, the adoption must be started from scratch.

"No!" Tim screeched when I called him at work with the news. "I served for twelve years in the Army with top-secret security clearance. They took my fingerprints *once*. In my *career*."

I kept my voice emotionless. Only one of us could lose control and right now that person was Tim. "There were two sets of prints. Only mine were lost."

Tim took a few deep breaths. In the background, I heard one of the nurses calling him. "Dr. Berger, Dr. Berger."

"This is insanity," he said. "I'll call and email every elected official in the state of California."

Tim went into high gear. He contacted our U.S. senator, our representative, and for good measure, my sister's high school friend, the ambassador. He explained that my fingerprints had been previously approved. He invited them to check my criminal record. I had none. They had no immediate solution except to promise to investigate the matter.

Tim made a bet that the adoption would be approved around New Year's and booked us three one-way tickets from Guatemala City to San Francisco on January 5. I scheduled a third print appointment with Márquez. I was relieved we had a strategy. There was still Olivia to care for, my child who depended on me for everything. I had to keep going.

I gave notice to our landlord and told Paola and Aracely that we would be gone at the end of December. Paola would continue in her position as housekeeper, but Aracely, I knew, would miss her work and the extra income. She had once told me that a position as *niñera* to adoptive mothers was highly coveted among locals because Americans paid wages three times higher than the going rate. I doubted I'd ever find a *niñera* more devoted. Never once had I worried about Olivia while she was in Aracely's care.

These were the last few days Olivia and I had alone together, and I dearly appreciated them. The weather was the best I'd seen. Courtyards were filled with blooming birds-of-paradise, and the red and pink geraniums in our window box were in full flower. Olivia waved to the boys who washed the cars, who bagged our groceries, who sold the orchids from the backs of their bicycles. Our daily routine felt like pure joy. We ate breakfast, chatted with Paola. Played on the Cathedral steps, walked to Conexión, met with Kendra and Susanna at La Fuente, and splashed around the fountain. Stopped for ice cream in the Square as we watched that day's parades. Swam at Hotel Antigua. Each day was a treasure.

Monday afternoon, nine days before Christmas, Olivia and I checked into the Camino Real after my third fingerprint sample was taken. We spent a few hours by the pool, waiting for Tim to arrive from San Francisco. He'd be with us for the pink slip, which we hoped would come on Christmas Eve.

"You still here?" the bellmen asked.

"What happened?" asked Belbeth, the concierge. "I thought you left long ago."

The other adoptive parents gazed at us with curiosity, and I imagined what they were thinking: *Why is that girl so big? She understands English. Are they here on a return visit?*

Olivia ran around the lobby like she owned the place. Either the staff members were excellent actors or they were truly delighted to see her. They regarded me with respect. She was almost two years old and I was still there. That counted for something.

That night, Tim strode into the lobby with the energy of someone ready to throw a punch. His first words to me were "This is bullshit."

"Tell me about it," I said, smiling as I leaned in for a kiss. He was angry enough for both of us. "Say hello to your daughter, honey. She's got her own Guatemalan passport."

Tim took Olivia from me and gave her a hug. "Hey, big girl. Daddy missed you."

He unhooked his backpack from his shoulders and dangled it

in front of me. "I've got a stack of emails in here from half the state officials in California. Everybody agrees this is royally messed up."

I took the backpack from him and massaged his shoulder. Messed up didn't begin to describe it.

The next morning, Tim and I opted not to eat our usual quick bite in the ninth-floor adoption lounge, but to eat a fancier breakfast in the restaurant. It was around 7 AM, and we were wearing our swimsuits under our sweatpants and T-shirts. After we ate, we'd take advantage of the Camino Real's pool and alternate swimming laps while the other played with Olivia.

We chose a table near the front of the restaurant in order to disturb the fewest number of diners, and when the waiter came up, I ordered yogurt and granola, and a serving of bacon and eggs for Olivia. Tim was still undecided, and asked the waiter to return in a minute or two. As he perused his menu, I bounced Olivia on my lap and watched a stream of well-dressed businesspeople approach the maître d's station and request to be seated. They blended into a generic blur of men in suits and women in high heels when suddenly the face of one of them came into focus: Mandy Márquez. She must have been on her way to the Embassy. When she reached the head of the line, the maître d' handed her a brown paper bag and a container of coffee, as though she were a regular customer with a standing order. Márquez smiled as she opened her purse for her wallet. Out from behind Door #8, she seemed much more human and approachable.

"Tim." I shook his wrist and nodded toward Márquez.

"Ask her to join us," Tim said.

With Olivia in my arms, I slid off my chair and stood by the front door. "Remember me?" I said.

Márquez looked over Olivia's head in the direction of Tim. "How could I forget?"

"Do you have a minute to sit down?"

"I honestly don't." But she moved toward our table anyway, her coffee in one hand and brown bag in the other. I stood beside her with Olivia on my hip.

"I'm sorry for all this, folks," said Márquez.

"Eh," Tim said. He leaned in confidentially and continued in a stage whisper. "I was in the military. I know how it is."

"Really?" Márquez's face brightened. "My brother's a Marine."

"Tough guys, Marines," Tim said. "I was in the Army."

Márquez glanced around the restaurant as though she was looking for someone, or someone was looking for her. She returned her attention to Tim. "About the fingerprints," she said. "The Embassy doesn't advertise this, but we do give waivers."

Tim raised his eyebrows. He was good at not rushing in to fill a silence, allowing the other person to take whatever time they need to complete a thought.

The brown bag rustled in Márquez's hand. "Your regional immigration office can fax a letter verifying you have no criminal record." She tightened her grip on her container of coffee. "I didn't tell you this."

Tim tapped his closed fist against his heart and bowed his head.

"Thank you," he said.

The next Monday afternoon, I helped Olivia drip sand over the bottom of the slide at Hotel Antigua as Tim sat on a swing, watching us. On the lawn a few yards away, the groundskeepers dismantled an enormous yellow-and-white striped tent, the site of an extravagant wedding on Sunday evening. The hotel's four resident parrots squawked in the olive tree, calling out to answer the splashes and shouts from the kids in the pool. Against the backdrop of Antigua's triumvirate of volcanoes—Agua, Fuego, and Acatenango—the sky was a heavenly light blue described perfectly in Spanish, *celeste*.

My phone rang. Mandy Márquez. I turned away from Olivia and Tim so I could fully concentrate on what she was telling me. Our request for a waiver had been approved. We needed to come to the Embassy Tuesday morning to pick up our paperwork. Our pink slip would be issued on Christmas Eve.

I clicked off the phone and turned back to my family. "We did it," I said. "They gave us the waiver."

Tim stood up from the swing and pumped his fists in the air. I rushed toward him with such momentum that we toppled backward. Laughing, we both reached for Olivia and hugged her between us. Olivia, our daughter.

Chapter 20

FAMILY

Because of Olivia, everything else in my life finally made sense. My failed first marriage. My early menopause. The sequence of boyfriends who had rejected me because of my infertility. Meeting Tim. All of it had had a single purpose: To lead me to her.

My parents welcomed Olivia with open arms. Family and friends clamored to meet her. She was the undisputed star of every social gathering. I felt more settled and happy than I ever remembered.

After Olivia had been home for eight months, I asked Tim how he felt about adopting a little boy. First, because my sisters and brother and I were very close, and I wanted that for our daughter. And second, because I didn't want Olivia to be the only "adopted Guatemalan" in our family. That seemed too big a label for one child to bear. Tim didn't hesitate. *Yes.*

Our son was born to a different birth mother in November 2004. His birth name was "Carlos," but we called him Mateo. Mateo was not indigenous, but *Ladino*—so light that his birth certificate listed his skin color as "*blanco.*" Only four pounds six ounces at birth, he was tiny and small-boned, with eyebrows so bushy that my brother dubbed him "Martin Scorsese." We used an east coast agency that I had learned about through Sofía. Our second experience was similar to that of most Americans adopting from Guatemala: We visited once for a weekend and never left the hotel. Mateo was home in six months.

Temperamentally, Mateo was very different from Olivia: easy-going where Olivia was intense, noisy where she was quiet, affectionate where she was aloof. Whether this was because of who he was by nature, or because he had lived with a single, devoted foster mother since birth, we'd never know. But it pained me to think that Olivia may have suffered in some way because of her complicated early experiences. She remained a fiercely independent child, resistant to affection. I called her an "old soul."

The concept of "attachment" continued to have special meaning for us as an adoptive family. More than anything, Tim and I wanted Olivia to feel attached to us as her parents. We knew she loved us, but a part of her still felt withheld. Ultimately, the challenge of dealing with the situation led us to seek professional help. We began weekly meetings with a child psychologist, which we continued for more than three years. The psychologist stressed how important it was for Tim and me to be consistent with Olivia, to make her feel safe, to set boundaries and limits, and to reinforce any affectionate behavior she showed. We worked hard at all of it, and gradually, with time, Olivia softened. Having Mateo for a brother helped. A sweet, happy, exuberant boy, he idolized Olivia, and was generous with hugs and kisses. Eventually, Olivia became less cautious and reserved, and more trusting and loving. When her first-grade teacher described Olivia as "friendly" and "social," we were jubilant. The reading, math, and science we could teach her. Connecting with others was what we considered paramount.

We'd found our best friends in the adoption community. Kendra and Susanna lived in Guatemala a full year longer than we did. Eighteen months to our nearly six. After a year of no responses to his public notices in the newspaper, her *notario* created a new birth certificate for Susanna's birth mother, so she appeared to be eighteen. Kendra agreed to the false birth certificate as a last resort, but the decision haunted her. We spoke by phone as she was boarding the airplane home, and she said, "I don't know this country anymore." She had no desire to visit Guatemala again. I felt as close to Kendra as I did to women I'd known since childhood; Olivia and Susanna considered each other sisters. Heather remained in regular contact; we met every summer in Colorado. Two little girls in Olivia's school were adopted from Guatemala. One was born in Momostenango, a village not far from Totonicapán, and the other from Flores. Their mothers and I discussed our children's development with much more candor than we did with other parents.

If I knew someone was adopted, I made a point of mentioning it to our children: Steve Jobs, Faith Hill, Jamie Foxx, Dave Thomas, and Kristin Chenoweth were adopted, as were Jamie Lee Curtis's kids, the sons of Madonna and Emma Thompson, and some of Steven Spielberg's brood. People we knew from other contexts—preschool teachers and soccer coaches, physicians and shoe salesmen—confided in me that they were adopted, or their child was, or a cousin or uncle. Adoptees were so omnipresent in our lives that once, after I had introduced Olivia to two boys born in Russia, she looked at me with exasperation and said, "I know, Mom. *Everyone's adopted.*"

In our world, everyone was.

In the summer, we went to Latin American Heritage Camp, where our kids met and played and learned with other kids born in Central and South America. The first day, Olivia looked around with awe at the assembled group and said, "Everyone here looks like me." Olivia studied Spanish after school. We sought out Latino families on the playground and at church.

Our house was filled with Guatemalan artwork and textiles. We followed Guatemalan politics and read books on the country's history. After Olivia's adoption was finalized, we rented a car and took a two-week road trip all over Guatemala, returning to California in January. Our first stop was Totonicapán. We drove to Panajachel, Lake Atitlán, and Chichicastenango. By small airplane, we visited the Mayan ruins at Tikal. Olivia may not have remembered most of the trip, but we had scrapbooks to remind her.

Pictures also reminded Olivia of her foster mother, Lupe, and the Garza family, to whom we said our final goodbyes in the Camino Real lobby. The meeting was bittersweet because Olivia refused to get off my lap to greet them. The Garzas left after an awkward half hour. For years afterward, Olivia would look at Lupe's picture and ask who she was, as though she were seeing her foster mother for the first time. My theory was that the memory of being separated from Lupe was so painful that Olivia was forced to repress it. I wish I had known how to better handle the arrangement. I'm not sure I would know even now.

Among friends and acquaintances, I became known as a source of information about adoption. If someone was thinking of adopting, he or she wanted to talk to me, or, better, visit us at home to experience our family up close. A friend from college, now a university professor, adopted a three-year-old daughter from foster care after meeting Olivia and Mateo. Another couple who knew us adopted a little boy from Kazakhstan after years of infertility treatments. Far-flung friends emailed: "I have a friend who's thinking about adoption. Can they call you?"

Complete strangers felt free to comment. A woman in the grocery store saw me with Mateo and asked, "What is he mixed with? Korean?" A girl at church turned around in her pew and asked Olivia, "How come you're black and your mother's white?"

Once, a man accosted me in the fixtures aisle of Home Depot. "Where are they from?" he asked. "Mexico?"

"Guatemala."

"Well," he said. "Let's hope they bring something good to this country, instead of just taking everything."

The questions and comments may have been intrusive, but they were usually not mean-spirited. People were curious. Despite the prevalence of adoption in this country, families like ours remained a distinct minority. Each interaction was an opportunity to educate.

Many people had told me they could never love a child they hadn't "created" themselves. Because I'd never been pregnant, I didn't know what creating another life felt like. But I could say this: I loved my children more than I ever imagined possible. I would have walked through fire for them. In fact, while I sometimes described myself as an "adoptive mother," I never called them my "adopted" children. They were my children. End of sentence. Adoption was the way we became a family.

In most international adoptions, contact with birth mothers was impossible because little information was known. In Guatemalan adoption, however, most families had access to a birth mother's name and *cédula* number—a national identity card—at a minimum. We possessed that information about Ana. It would be possible to hire someone to find her.

I asked Tim what he thought. He considered his reply. "Our lives are going so well," he said. "What if we learn something we don't want to know?"

Our local bookstore hosted a book-signing for the writer A. M. Homes, who met her biological parents at the age of thirty-one and had written a memoir about it. As I sat in the audience and listened to her read the first chapter, I became uncomfortable as she described her intense sadness at being denied access to her biological roots for so many years. She depicted a childhood and adolescence that was shrouded in secrets and mystery, calling herself a loner who had trouble fitting in. She related scenes of a tortured young adulthood, when she developed elaborate fantasies of her birth parents. Forming a relationship with her birth mother (who died soon after Ms. Homes had met her) and birth father allowed her to feel some measure of closure.

After the reading, I waited at the end of the book-signing line to speak with her.

"My daughter is almost six," I said as she signed her name with a flourish. "Adopted from Guatemala."

"Oh?"

"Do you think I should try to find her birth mother?"

She stared at me as if to ask, "Have you not listened to anything I just read?"

My face reddened. "Or I should say, 'At what age should I look for her?' When Olivia is older?"

Ms. Homes set down her pen. "Your daughter deserves to know where she comes from. Find her mother as soon as possible."

Scrutiny of Guatemalan adoption increased. Rumors of kidnapped babies, falsified documents, and payments to birth mothers leaked out from the adoption community into the world beyond, until the subject became news too big to ignore. A front-page story in the *New York Times* labeled Guatemala a "virtual baby farm," where infants had become a "commodity." The article stated that baby finders "ply the Guatemalan countryside," seeking women who are willing to sell their children.

One night, Tim came home to find me on the family room sofa surrounded by a pile of used tissues. I was watching a television newsmagazine about adoption practices in Guatemala. Much of the show was shot with hidden cameras in the shadowy hallways of a "baby hotel," which I recognized as the Camino Real. The report focused on one particular "broker," a nefarious character who kidnapped babies from their Guatemalan mothers and sold them to unsuspecting, infertile couples in the United States. Although the "broker" had been banned from facilitating adoptions by the U.S. Embassy, unscrupulous agencies continued to use him.

Tim stared at the TV screen in disbelief. "That's Theodore," he said.

The woman who would search for Ana went by the initial "D." Her fee was $1,200. She lived in Antigua, in one of the posh neighborhoods on the north side. I contacted her right before Christmas. We communicated via email. Her English was superb. She wrote that she had been motivated to start searching because she worried about birth mothers who relinquished their children and never heard from them again.

"The mothers live in extreme poverty. They have no power over their lives. They don't plan for adoption. It just happens."

I didn't ask: If you are so concerned about birth mothers, why do you charge so much? I only wanted to know: Can you get the job done?

D seemed like she could. Of the 163 searches she had conducted, 160 had been successful. A dozen women in my adoption online community had used her services and recommended her highly.

When D learned Olivia's birth mother was from Totonicapán, she explained that people in highland indigenous communities were so suspicious of outsiders that it was very dangerous for her to conduct searches there. Not only for her, but for the birth mothers. A few months earlier, four women believed to have relinquished their children had been forced to kneel on crushed rock while their heads were shaved. A month later, a mob lashed and shaved the heads of twelve others because they were believed to be associated with adoptions.

Discretion was crucial. While conducting a search, D knocked on the birth mother's door carrying an express mail envelope, pretending to be a courier with news from the United States. Because many Guatemalans had relatives living in the U.S., this was plausible. For security, she was accompanied by her husband, who distracted the birth mother's husband or boyfriend while D explained why she had come.

"The man who lives with her usually doesn't know about the child. If he finds out, he is afraid she will give away his child, too," D wrote. "Often he will beat her."

I warned D that we had tried to find Ana ourselves, when we visited Totonicapán, but couldn't find the address.

"That information is false to protect the identity of the birth mother," D answered. "I've researched cases where it is the location of an empty lot, or a tree."

Because of the danger to herself and the birth mothers, D was about to suspend her searches in indigenous communities in the highlands, but I had reached her just in time. Her very last search was for Ana in Totonicapán.

In February 2008, an email arrived. D had found Ana, and Ana had agreed to meet me. I flew to Guatemala over President's Day weekend to meet D in Antigua. The trip felt like a homecoming: the smell of bus exhaust on the road from the capital, women carrying baskets on their heads, men repairing the cobblestone streets. It was summer in Guatemala, as hot as it ever got in the Land of Eternal Spring, and Antigua was crawling with tourists. They crowded around the fountain with their faces tilted toward the sun, grateful to have escaped the snow and ice back home. D and I sat on a bench, our backs warmed by the sun.

"When I told Ana I had an envelope and pictures of Stefany Mishell, she lunged toward me, as if to grab them from my hands," D said. "She studied the pictures for a long time. She is very Catholic, with an altar in her bedroom. She called my visit *un milagro*, a miracle."

D spoke in a quiet, cultured voice. Her pale skin was speckled with cinnamon-colored freckles. Her hand, when I shook it, was soft and buttery; the hand of a woman who had never washed a dish or mopped a floor. She was married to a successful businessman, with two daughters at the country's premier private university. I had been afraid she might be yet another opportunist in the lucrative adoption business. But in person, she was thoughtful and deliberate, her expression kind.

"Ana lives in one of the most primitive circumstances I have seen," D said. "It was difficult for us to communicate. Her first language is K'iché, with just minimal understanding of Spanish."

D had found Ana by asking at the municipal building in Totonicapán. The clerk there had known Ana's parents; her family had been in Toto for generations. In the section of town where they lived, there were no street names or house numbers.

D pulled out a small envelope of pictures for me, taken at Ana's home. She selected one, a photograph of a mud hut with a corrugated aluminum roof. In the backyard were two scrawny brown hens and a drooping clothesline strung between two trees.

D allowed me to examine the photo before she spoke.

"After Ana's husband died, she took in laundry to support herself and her two children. She also climbs into the mountains and chops wood."

It was hard to absorb that Olivia's birth family lived in such a grim setting. They had electricity, but no stove. D showed pictures of the spartan interior, including a blackened area in the small kitchen where Ana cooked over an open fire. I'd traveled enough to understand that material belongings didn't guarantee happiness. I also knew that certain basics made life easier.

"How are the children doing?" I asked. "Olivia's half-siblings."

"Her son, Luis, is fifteen. He is learning to be a carpenter, like her late husband. Her daughter, Dulce, is eleven. She does not attend school, perhaps because Ana cannot afford to pay for books. They weren't home when I visited."

D shuffled through her photos. "Ana's father is also dead, but her mother is alive. She lives with Ana, and knows about the birth of Stefany Mishell. I didn't want to be impolite by asking for her mother's picture, but my husband snapped one when she wasn't looking."

A view of a very small woman from the back, walking away on a dusty footpath. Olivia's biological grandmother.

"What about Ana?" I asked. "Were you able to take her picture?"

D smiled as she reminded me that the Maya did not like having their photographs taken. "I asked politely of Ana and she reluctantly agreed. Then as I pressed the shutter, Ana raised her arms overhead to fix her hair." D lifted her own arms to demonstrate. "I didn't want to ask again."

She passed me a blurry, out-of-focus photo of a wispy figure with her arms in the air. I made out long black hair and an embroidered blouse, an altar in the background, a dirt floor. The shape of the long, narrow face was the same as Olivia's.

D had arranged for the three of us to meet on Tuesday at noon in Panajachel, four hours northwest of Antigua on the southern shore of Lake Atitlán. Pana, as it was called by everyone, was close enough to Totonicapán that Ana could ride the bus, but far enough away that no one would recognize her. Besides Ana's mother, only her sister knew about Ana's pregnancy. I could also be invisible, blending in easily with the light-skinned backpackers who used Panajachel as a starting point from which to explore the rugged highlands.

On Monday, D was conducting another search in the nearby town of Xela. She planned to pick up Ana at the bus stop. At noon, they would meet me at a taco stand on the beach at the end of the main tourist street, Calle Santander.

"I'm not sure Ana uses a fork," D said. "Better that she feels comfortable to use her hands eating a taco."

I knew Pana fairly well. During our road trip, Tim and I had stayed for a week, using it as our home base from which to explore other towns around Lake Atitlán. Like Antigua, it was a tourist destination, teeming with souvenir shops and local handicrafts, hotels and restaurants. I was not concerned about finding my way around. What I was nervous about was meeting Ana. After I gave her an update on Olivia, what would we talk about?

"I have done this countless times, with many birth mothers and parents," D assured me. "The conversation will go smoothly. I'll be with you."

She patted my cheek with her soft palm as we said goodbye.

I spent Monday night at a small hotel in the village of San Marcos, on the eastern shore of the lake, in sight of Atitlán's three magnificent volcanoes. San Marcos was much smaller than Pana, its population an interesting blend of indigenous locals and transient backpackers who studied alternative therapies at the holistic center. It felt like the ideal spot to spend the night before such a meaningful day: in the middle of nowhere, with nothing to do but soak up the ambient meditative calm.

Before going to bed, I called Tim to say goodnight to him, Mateo, and Olivia. I didn't tell my daughter that the next day I was

meeting Ana, and that someday, she might, too. For as long as possible, I wanted to keep Olivia to myself. I wanted to remain the center
of her small universe, her only mother.

Tuesday morning I was awakened by the sound of roosters. I hurried to the lake for a quick swim before heading off to a restaurant
for breakfast. Back in my hotel room, I spent fifteen minutes debating
which outfit to wear: one of my colorful Guatemalan skirts from my
Antigua days? Or the khaki pants and long-sleeved shirt that instantly
identified me as American? I opted to go with the obvious American.

By 10:30 AM, I was at the dock on the beach, waiting to catch the
lancha for the boat ride to Pana. I felt jumpy and fidgety, as if I were
meeting a blind date. I desperately wanted Ana to like me. But more than
that, I wanted her to understand how much Tim and I cherished Olivia.

My cell phone rang.

"I have contracted something horrible in Xela," D rasped.

"Something you ate?"

"Not from eating. Influenza."

The *lancha* chugged up to the dock. The pilot jumped off to
secure it with a rope. A few passengers clambered off; the waiting
passengers scuffled past me and climbed aboard.

"I can't meet you," D said. "You must meet her yourself."

"How will we communicate?"

"You will know what to say. She will wait for you at the gasoline
station. Across from the bus stop."

Like everything else in the adoption, this was a step I would have to figure out for myself. I took a deep breath and jumped onto the *lancha*.

The boat slid neatly against the dock in Pana. I was the first passenger off. I scurried up the planked gangway and onto the paved street. Kiosks selling cell phone cards and freshly squeezed lemonade lined one side. A few yards ahead, three Guatemalan men plodded into town, one using a cross-country ski pole as a walking stick. I fell in behind them. It was eleven thirty, and the sun blazed down so hot that the air felt as thick as cotton. I quickened my pace to catch the ski pole. Except for me, nobody was moving fast.

"*Por favor?*"

The men turned toward me. They were old and skinny, with bowed legs. They each wore a ranchero hat. The man with the ski pole wore a rope for a belt.

"*El autobús?*" I made a motion for a steering wheel. "*De* Totonicapán?"

"*El autobús de Totonicapán?*" The ski pole man pushed back his ranchero hat. His knuckles were as thick as walnuts. He lifted his ski pole and thrust it forward. "*Adelante.*"

Up ahead. I should have known. I bowed slightly as I glided by them. "*Gracias.*"

The men touched the brims of their hats.

D had said that the Maya didn't keep calendars or wear watches so I shouldn't be surprised if Ana didn't appear on time, or at all. I didn't slow down. Somehow I had sensed that Ana would defy D's expectations and arrive early. I didn't want to be the one who was late.

I reached the end of the street. On the right hand side, a gas station.

And sitting on the curb out front, with her feet in the gutter and her chin in her hands, was Ana. I recognized her because her profile was identical to Olivia's.

She was dressed in a purple skirt and cotton *huipil* that was embroidered on every inch. Her frilly apron was also intricately embroidered. Although her clothes were faded and threadbare, she was, I was sure, dressed in her very best outfit.

Ana saw me and stood up. She was taller than I had expected, although I shouldn't have been surprised. Olivia was tall. Ana wore brown plastic sandals with low heels. Her skin was the color of nutmeg.

When I reached her, she looked directly into my face. Her eyes were Olivia's eyes, brown and piercing. She had the same elegant ears.

"*Soy la mamá de Stefany Mishell*," Ana said. She smiled, showing large teeth capped with gold. Her handshake was strong.

"*Yo también*," I answered. "Me too."

I felt as if I were looking at my daughter in thirty years. I'd never seen Olivia reflected this way. It was both exhilarating and shocking.

"You are the same as my daughter."

I was so shaken up by their close resemblance, I stumbled over the simple words. "I'm sorry. My Spanish is not good."

"*My* Spanish is not good."

She spoke with an accent I'd never heard before, which I realized must be K'iché. We were both using our second language.

"How was your trip?" I asked. "Are you hungry?" My voice quavered. I was on the verge of tears.

Ana reached for my hand and held it.

We turned toward Calle Santander to find a restaurant, still holding hands, as though walking together down a street in Panajachel was the most natural occurrence in the world. We passed some picnic tables where four Mayan women in red skirts and blouses were eating lunch. No comment from them, or us.

"Do you like pizza?" I asked.

I suddenly didn't want to eat at a taco stand on the beach the way D had suggested. I wanted this meal to be special. We turned into an Italian restaurant with red-and-white checkered cloths on the tables and frescoes of gondolas on the walls. Instead of the ubiquitous peppers and onions, the place smelled of garlic. A group of Canadian tourists dressed in maple leaf T-shirts had claimed five tables. Two American couples filled another one. Ana and I sat at a booth next to the front door. She was the only person dressed in *traje* in the restaurant, and I wasn't sure the snooty waiter who'd ushered us to our table would have let her sit down if she wasn't with me.

Ana ate her pizza solemnly, with a knife and fork. I followed her lead, cutting mine, too. We sipped our Cokes through straws. We ate the entire meal in silence, observing each other discreetly. Ana's hands were shaped just like Olivia's, down to her fingernails. Their noses sloped at the same angle. I was aware how different I was from both of them.

The waiter cleared away our plates. I asked him to wrap the remaining pizza so I could give it to Ana to take home. Taking home food was not customary in Guatemala, but I didn't want Ana to see me waste a crumb. For the same reason, I slurped every drop of my soda.

"We changed the name of Stefany," I said when the waiter left. "It is now Olivia."

"Olivia?"

"We weren't sure you gave her the name Stefany Mishell."

She didn't answer. I couldn't tell if she was upset or simply mulling over new information.

"We thought Yolanda gave her the name," I added.

Ana looked puzzled, as though not sure who "Yolanda" was.

"*Stefany Mishell es un nombre bonito,*" Ana said finally.

"Is it fine that her name is Olivia?" I pressed.

"Olivia is also a nice name."

I let the subject drop. I told her that Olivia was very intelligent. And tall. I held my hand up from the floor to give Ana an approximation. As much as I wanted to tell her about Olivia's life—her outstanding school, the nearby playgrounds, her favorite toys—to do so seemed insensitive. Ana's collarbones jutted out from the neckline of her blouse. Her wrists were half the size of mine. For her to know that Olivia was healthy and eating regularly was enough.

The waiter returned with the wrapped pizza and set it on the table. I paid the check.

Ana and I gazed out the window to Calle Santander. The shadows had grown longer.

The Canadian tourists were noisily negotiating their bill, arguing over who ordered what. The waiter leaned against the wall by the kitchen door, periodically peeking over the top of his newspaper to observe the discussion. The Americans were inspecting a map.

I turned to Ana. "How did you meet Yolanda?" I asked casually.

She looked confused.

"Yolanda, from Los Angeles." No response. "Or Theodore? From the hotel?"

She shook her head. "I don't know them."

I tried another tactic. "How did you decide to place Olivia for adoption, then?"

Ana reached into the top of her *huipil* and pulled out a frayed fabric purse. She unzipped the purse and pulled out a wrinkled, much-handled, two-inch head shot of a very young, very handsome man in a military uniform.

"This is my husband who died."

The father of her other two children, Luis and Dulce. The social worker's report stated he had been killed in a carpentry accident, but I always wondered if he was killed in the country's thirty-six-year civil war. The war ended in 1996, so the timing would have been right. Clearly he had been a soldier, but I didn't know enough about Guatemalan military uniforms to interpret the significance of the one he was wearing. What I did know was that the military drove through indigenous villages like Toto and forced every able-bodied man to enlist.

I gave her back the photo. "He is a handsome man. Very young."

She offered no reason for his early death. Instead, she tucked the purse with the photo inside back into her blouse, then cast her eyes downward and stared at the table. When she spoke, her voice was almost a whisper.

"After my husband died, it was difficult for me to support my family. I had two children and my mother to care for. I worked hard. I knew a man in my village. When I became pregnant, he didn't want to be the father."

She glanced up quickly, her eyes hooded with concern. "I don't want to tell this to Stefany because it may be hurtful to her."

I nodded slowly, to show I understood. "Can you tell me his name?"

She glanced furtively side to side to make sure no one except me was listening. In a whisper, she said his name. She bit her lip and lowered her eyes again.

"I could not remain in Toto. I moved to San Lucas Sacatepéquez to live with a friend. We both worked as housekeepers. I had the baby in the public hospital in Antigua. After she was born, I didn't know what to do. My husband is dead. I couldn't go back to Toto with a child."

Ana covered her face with her hands for a long moment before she continued.

"I kept the baby for eight days. Then I gave her to my friend."

Her explanation was so straightforward, I almost couldn't believe what I was hearing. She'd had a baby she couldn't take care of, and she'd made a hard decision. Not easy, not without great pain. But simple.

"Did your friend give the baby to Yolanda?"

"I don't know. I moved back to Toto. I didn't see the baby for a year, until a woman named Gilda drove to my house. She took me to the capital to prove I'm the baby's mother. The baby sat on my lap. She was already a big girl."

Her voice trailed off. "I never saw her again."

She lifted her chin higher, as though to strengthen her resolve. "Now I know she is alive. I don't have to worry."

"Would you like me to give Olivia a message from you?"

Ana didn't stop to think before she answered. "Tell her I love her. She is of my blood."

I felt a sharp sting in my eyes. The tears I had been suppressing flooded out. As much as Olivia belonged to me, she belonged to

Ana. As much as she was Ana's, she was mine. Their loss was something I would never understand. Their wound was something I may never heal. I was mourning for birth mothers everywhere, for the choices they made for the sake of their children. I was mourning for Guatemala, the beautiful and flawed country that would always be a part of Olivia.

Ana stood and moved over to my chair. She put her arms around me as though comforting a child. "Don't cry, *mamalita*," she said.

Olivia with her birth mother and grandmother in February 2009.

~~~~~~

Olivia and her family in 2010.

EPILOGUE

A year later to the day, I returned to Guatemala with Olivia. Tim stayed home with Mateo. My oldest sister, Patrice, who is Olivia's godmother, accompanied us.

Except from pictures Olivia had seen of the country, she didn't remember anything. The place seemed completely different to me, too. Adoptions had been shut for almost two years, and we were the only Americans at the Camino Real, the only adoptive family we saw in Antigua. Everywhere we went, we felt people watching us. I didn't let Olivia out of my sight.

Once again, D arranged a meeting for us with Ana in Panajachel. Olivia, Patrice, and I spent the night before in a hotel on Lake Atitlán. Olivia had a book of photos to share with Ana, and planned to show Ana some of her best drawings. Olivia wanted to be an artist.

Although I'd been preparing Olivia for this meeting for months, I wasn't sure she understood what it meant. But in the morning before we left, she paused as she put on her hair-band.

"So I have two mommies," she said. "You mommy and Mamá Ana."

"That's right," I said, smoothing her hair. Olivia nodded. "More people to love," she said.

ACKNOWLEDGMENTS

Many, many people helped me during the five years I spent writing *Mamalita*. I am grateful to each and every one of them.

Thank you to my agent, Jenni Ferrari-Adler, for her faith in this book from first reading. Thank you to my editor at Seal Press, Brooke Warner, for loving the story and shepherding it into the world. Also at Seal, I am grateful to Krista Lyons, Donna Galassi, Eva Zimmerman, Krissa Lagos, Sarah Juckniess, Jane Musser, and Lisa Lee.

The Community of Writers at Squaw Valley made me believe I was capable of writing a book. Thank you to Brett Hall Jones, Sands Hall, Andrew Tonkovich, and Steve Susoyev, and to my creative nonfiction groups led by Anthony Swofford and Peter Steinberg. You provided the perfect combination of criticism and encouragement.

I am indebted to Book Passage in Corte Madera, California, where I enrolled in every writing class offered and found a creative home. Special thanks to Dawn Yun and the Writing Mamas for never once saying to me, "You're still writing that book?" as the years went by and I continued to grapple with the manuscript. Thanks, too, to Linda Watanabe McFerrin for commenting after every chapter, "I can't wait to read what happens next." My Friday night writing group, "the Shrinks"—so named because everyone except me is a mental health professional—not only kept me accountable to bring in pages but also supplied unlimited free therapy. Everyone should be so lucky. Cheers to Lorrie Goldin, Avvy Mar, Gale Lipsyte, and Molly Delaney.

My teacher, mentor, and friend, Joyce Maynard, guided me during workshops in her homes in Guatemala and California. Watching Joyce at her whiteboard as she deconstructed a sentence or a scene taught me how those elements functioned, and how I could best use them in the service of the story. I learned so much by observing how Joyce thinks. Thank you, thank you.

I am grateful to writers I met through Joyce in Guatemala. Robert Bausch listened as I struggled to distill the essence of the narrative arc, while Laura Lippman helped me better understand the mechanics of pacing. I am also indebted to Andi Sciacca for helping me find my way into the story and to the other participants who experienced some of it along with me. Thank you to Kimberle López, Michel Salazar-Linden, Nancy Hoffman, David Corbett, Helmut Soto, and Sister Kris Schrader for their insights into Guatemalan history, politics, and grammar.

Early readers of parts or all of the manuscript helped me to hone it. Many thanks to Janis Cooke Newman, Adair Lara, Tom Jenks, Alice B. Acheson, and B. Lynn Goodwin. Other readers included Greg Stebner, Suzanne Weiss, Marianne Lonsdale, Laura-Lynne Powell, Tina Bournazos, Jennifer O'Shaughnessy, Julia Fulton, Leceta Chisholm Guibault, Svetlana Nikitina, and the late Ruth Scott. Also, Kallie Kull, Gretchen B. Wright, Anne Sigmon, Jane Lamont, Jill Pixley, and Sharon Murphy. Your comments helped.

Of the many books that informed this project, Daniel Wilkinson's *Silence on the Mountain*, Héctor Pérez-Brignoli's *A Brief History of Central America*, Beatriz Manz's *Paradise in Ashes*, and Elizabeth Bell's *Antigua Guatemala: The City and Its Heritage* were particularly helpful. I am grateful to Alison Biggar of the *San Francisco Chronicle Magazine* and Mark Trautwein of KQED-FM for publishing my first essays. The Marin County Public Library system provided quiet space and needed resources.

I cherish the support of good friends during the adoption and over the years it took to complete this book, including Lisa Troland, Sharon McCarthy, Heidi McKinley, Laura Craighead Reich, Jenny Sewall, Ulrika Brand, Sandy Wilmot, Helen Dunn, Jean Cotterell, and Rob Sherwin from the east coast; and Synthia Malina, Jini Bernstein Archibald, Jill Jones Mason, Bethany Nelson, Penny Taylor, Diana Gaston, Emilia Belotti, Sue Sullivan, Anne Farrell, and Marcia Banks from the west. In the Bay Area, special thanks to Dr. Bruce and Marya Wintroub, Dr. Kimberly Keough, and Dr. Seth Matarasso, and to my friends at the San Francisco Museum of Modern Art and the University of California San Francisco.

My parents, Bob and Gerry O'Dwyer; my siblings, Patrice and Robert O'Dwyer, Adrienne Phillips, and Deanna O'Dwyer-Swensen; and their spouses and children have stood by me as a limitless source of love and support. I am grateful to them, as well as to Yvonne Berger and the entire Berger clan.

To the adoptive families I've met—before, during, and after our adoption—and especially the mothers who fostered with me in Antigua: The bond I feel with you is lasting and strong. May your families be healthy and thrive. To the people in Guatemala who helped us complete the adoption: May God keep you in the palm of His hand.

Finally, I thank my husband, Tim Berger, and our children, Olivia and Mateo. Every day, your unconditional love shows me the true meaning of family.

ABOUT THE AUTHOR

Jessica O'Dwyer is the adoptive mother to a daughter and son, both born in Guatemala. Her essays have been published in the *San Francisco Chronicle Magazine, Adoptive Families,* the *West Marin Review,* and KQED-FM *Perspectives.* Jessica lives with her husband and children in Northern California. Visit her at www.mamalitathebook.com.

© LISA VAILLANCOURT

SELECTED TITLES FROM SEAL PRESS

For more than thirty years, Seal Press has published

groundbreaking books. By women. For women.

Navigating the Land of If: Understanding Infertility and Exploring Your Options, by Melissa Ford. $16.95, 978-1-58005-262-7. Melissa Ford presents readers with a guide for navigating the complex world of infertility, whether they're trying to get pregnant or seeking alternative options.

Choosing You: Deciding to Have a Baby on My Own, by Alexandra Soiseth. $15.95, 1-58005-222-3. The deeply honest memoir of one woman's decision to brave pregnancy and motherhood alone.

Motherhood and Feminism: Seal Studies, by Amber E. Kinser. $14.95, 978-1-58005-270-2. Author and mother Amber E. Kinser examines how the changing world of motherhood fits into feminist activism, and speculates on the future directions of these identities.

The Maternal Is Political: Women Writers at the Intersection of Motherhood and Social Change, edited by Shari MacDonald Strong. $15.95, 978-1-58005-243-6. Exploring the vital connection between motherhood and social change, The Maternal Is Political features thirty powerful literary essays by women striving to make the world a better place for children and families—both their own and other women's.

A Thousand Sisters: My Journey into the Worst Place on Earth to Be a Woman, by Lisa Shannon, foreword by Zainab Salbi. $24.95, 978-1-58005-296-2. Through her inspiring story of turning what started as a solo 30-mile run to raise money for Congolese women into a national organization, Run for Congo Women, Lisa Shannon sounds a deeply moving call to action for each person to find in them the thing that brings meaning to a wounded world.

Girls' Studies: Seal Studies, by Elline Lipkin. $14.95, 978-1-58005-248-1. A look at the socialization of girls in today's society and the media's influence on gender norms, expectations, and body image.

FIND SEAL PRESS ONLINE

www.SealPress.com

www.Facebook.com/SealPress

Twitter: @SealPress